BEHAVIOR INTERVENTION

WITHOUT

TEARS

Keeping FBAs and BIPs Simple

Terri Chiara Johnston

RESEARCH PRESS
PUBLISHERS

2612 North Mattis Avenue, Champaign, Illinois 61822
800.519.2707 / researchpress.com

RESEARCH PRESS
PUBLISHERS

PDF versions of forms included in this book are available for download on the book webpage at **www.researchpress.com/downloads**

Copies of this book may be ordered from Research Press at the address given on the title page.

Cover design by McKenzie Wagner, Inc.
Printed by Edwards Brothers Malloy

ISBN 978-0-87822-689-4
Library of Congress Control Number 2014941316

Contents

Figures

Acknowledgments

I am so fortunate to have a loving husband and family. Without them, I could never have made it through another "birthing" process writing this second book. Thanks especially to my husband, Joe Czup.

Particular thanks go to my friend Connie Kinner: You have been my biggest fan and a wonderful model of what a strong, capable woman can do in this world if she sets her mind to it. You have taught me to value exactly who I am and not bemoan who I am not. I am so very grateful to you.

Thanks, too, to my longtime friend Sandy Haltrich. There would never have been a book or a business without you.

Most of what I learned started at the Institute of Applied Behavior Analysis in California. Drs. Gary LaVigna and Thomas Willis were great mentors and helped me to develop my own paradigms so I could bring their wealth of knowledge into the reality of public schools. Thanks to you both.

Finally, thank you to Karen Steiner and Research Press. Karen, you are not only an excellent editor, you are also kind.

Prologue

This book is ready to go to print. I have read it over and over to be sure it's right. Unfortunately, I just can't let it go. There's something missing…something that will help pull the following chapters together for you.

My first book, *Data Without Tears* (Johnston, 2010), was easier. In that book, now in a second edition (Johnston, 2014), I was able to provide clear instructions for writing observable goals, objectives, and benchmarks for students with special needs. I also explained, as clearly as I was able, how to measure progress. Everything I talked about clustered around two main organizers. The first detailed the components that must be present in a measurable goal:

A = Audience

B = Behavior

C = Condition

D = Degree

The second consisted of a warning: Beware of C. R. A. P. data!

C.R.A.P.

Can't Rely on Any Part of It

In this book, I want to give you a map to guide you in the direction that will help the kids in your care. I want you to get to the point that you can do a functional behavior assessment immediately, so it becomes the way you recognize trouble before it starts and are able to keep problems small and manageable.

And that's what's challenging: The key difference between the two books is that THINKING is what's involved here, not following a model or filling in blanks. If I were with you when you're faced with a serious behavior problem that requires intervention, I would guide your thinking by asking a thousand questions, trying to get at what you see and perceive about the youngster. I would make sure that you were aware of your own biases about the student, the teacher, the classroom, the school, the parents…anything that might be coloring your ideas and judgments in ways that would interfere with developing a successful behavior intervention plan. You bring those biases to the assessment, good or bad, just as much as you bring all of your experience and training.

As you read through the case examples in this book, it won't be hard to see my own biases. So very much of the time, I have found that youngsters behave badly because they are such dismal failures at their work—academics. Kids know that it is always better to be bad than stupid, and finding that kids often use their inappropriate behavior to escape demands has probably been the most frequent result of the functional behavior assessments I've done. In defense of this bias, the teachers I have worked with have had miraculous results when following recommendations regarding academic instruction. Problematic behaviors disappeared and didn't return. So my bias has been upheld over time and experience.

However often this bias has led to a quick fix, solving academic problems does not always promote positive change. Another of my biases concerns my reluctance to accept that a student is acting out to seek attention. That is the LAST thing I look for, but sometimes it's the correct conclusion.

So here's your thinking map for creating FBAs and BIPs without too many tears:

1. Your perception is your own reality. How YOU perceive the problem will be how the plan will be written.

2. Your job, then, is to open yourself fully to the youngster's reality and how he or she perceives the world.

3. If you can do that, you can write an effective plan.

Start at the beginning and identify the behavior that is the most problematic. Collect good, reliable data and develop your hypothesis. Ask yourself and the educational team questions, keeping everyone focused on the behavior identified. Finally, develop a plan that addresses the problem proactively.

It really is that simple. Don't worry about forms—just focus on what the kid does and what he or she gets out of doing it that is such a problem for other people. Whatever the behavior is, it works: It gets the kid what he or she needs quickly and efficiently. Your job is to give the kid a better way to get what he or she needs.

So good luck. I know you're up to the task ahead of you.

1

Get It Straight

The Truth About Functional Behavior Assessments and the Law

When dealing with behavior challenges, prevention (regardless of who, what, when, or where) is the key. The only real way to help kids stop behaving inappropriately is to teach them new skills or alternative behaviors. The operative phrase here is "to teach." Not only do skills need to be taught, they need to be used consistently. "Therein lies the rub," as Hamlet said.

Too many times I've heard teachers say something like "He didn't make a good choice." What they mean is that the kid, regardless of being TOLD what to do time and time again, didn't do it. This viewpoint does not take into account what the kid wanted or needed at that point in time. If his needs were intense enough and outweighed what the school folks told him to do, or if the kid, despite being told, really didn't know HOW to demonstrate the desired behavior, "choosing" was never really much of an option.

So now we look at youngsters who, for whatever the reason, have behavior challenges compounding other learning problems—or, at the very least, have behavior challenges that coexist with some serious environmental issues that affect their ability to perform as adults want them to. For special education students, a mandated process exists to ensure that the purpose and effectiveness of subsequent interventions are documented systematically. The law reads as follows:

The Individuals with Disabilities Education Act (IDEA) requires (a) that the [Individual Education Program] team consider strategies, including positive interventions, to deal with behavior that interferes with the special education student's own learning or that of others (34 CFR 300.346(a)(2)); (b) that before a disciplinary removal of a special education student from school for more than 10 days in a school year, the IEP team must review an existing behavioral intervention plan (BIP) or, if none exists, conduct a functional behavioral assessment (FBA) and implement a BIP based on that FBA (34 CFR 300.520(b)); and (c) that if a child who has a BIP has been removed for more than 10 days is to be removed again (even for a one day suspension), the BIP must be reviewed and modified, if necessary (34 CFR 300.520(A)). These FBAs and BIPs must be committed to writing as documentary evidence that the school is in compliance with IDEA. (p. 9)

In my mind, this paragraph brings up critical points that can't be ignored:

1. This process is required for ALL special education students whose learning, because of his or her challenging behavior, is either compromised or compromises the learning of others. This is not a process to be used solely with students identified as severely emotionally disturbed or autistic.

2. Behavior plans must be written based on the information gathered during the FBA.

3. Behavior plans must be reviewed and modified periodically. That means plans need to grow and change with a student's needs. Once the student has learned and is consistently using an alternative behavior, and problem behaviors are either decreased or eliminated, new behaviors should be targeted. Then the IEP team should determine whether these behavioral support services are still needed.

4. Finally, the requirement to commit FBAs and BIPs in writing provides documentary evidence of compliance, resulting in a product. However, no consistent form or format is mandated.

Why This Book Now?

I just did a search on Amazon. Today, there are 1,012 books identified with the topic "functional behavior assessment" (I probably own 1,011 of them) and 765 with the topic "behavioral intervention plan." So why another one now?

Here's why: Most of these manuals present the functional behavior assessment (hereafter known as an FBA) and behavioral intervention plan (known from now on as a BIP) process as forms, interviews, checklists, procedures, and so forth that can make educators not only crazy but so overwhelmed with the thought of it that they give up before they begin. Am I right, or am I right? That's not to say that there aren't excellent resources out there because there are. In fact, in the references and bibliography of this book I list some of them so you can investigate them yourself.

However, I want to write a KISS book for you: Keep It Simple, Sweetheart! I want you to keep this book on your desk and pull it out frequently throughout the school year until you are able to think about behavior in a new way. I hope to change your *perception* of a youth's challenging behavior in such a way that you can conduct a mini-FBA in your head and immediately design intervention strategies that prevent problems from occurring altogether.

NOW who's crazy? I am no Pollyanna, believe me. Teaching is the hardest job in the world! I believe this with all my heart and soul. Lee Iacocca, former CEO of the Chrysler Corporation, puts it like this:

> In a completely rational society, the best of us would be teachers and the rest of us would have to settle for something less, because passing civilization along from one generation to the next ought to be the highest honor and the highest responsibility anyone could have. (Iacocca, n.d.)

Unfortunately, the best of us are having trouble juggling all the demands that teaching presents. No one can really appreciate how hard it is to be a good teacher without being in the classroom for a while. The time, effort, and resolve it takes to do this job well makes teaching more of a lifestyle than an occupation. And, ladies and gentlemen, that lifestyle can become a burden rather than the rewarding experience educators hoped for. This burden drives more than 30 percent of beginning teachers to leave the field within the first five years (Kopkowski, 2008). If you're looking at the stats for special education teachers, some think it's closer to 50 percent (Riggs, 2013).

Believe me, I know that lack of money can be a motivating factor for leaving the education field, but it isn't the number one reason people leave. According to many studies on the national and state levels, unbearable workloads and responsibilities related to meeting standards, and the deluge of paperwork associated with serving students with disabilities, frequently come in first. Safety, violence, and classroom management problems come in a close second. Money, poor working conditions, and lack of administrator support come in third or below (National Center for Education Statistics, Gonzalez & Brown, 2008).

Asher et al. (2010) remind us of another troubling fact: "Approximately one in four children and adolescents experience behavioral, developmental, emotional, or social and educational difficulties" (p. 1). One in four! So I'm writing this book to help teachers address challenging behaviors in their classroom successfully without a huge amount of unnecessary paperwork and rigmarole.

Positive behavior supports (PBS) are considered by state and federal educational agencies to be best practice when conducting FBAs and writing BIPs. The following chapters provide recommendations and examples that help keep the IDEA mandates not only efficient but effective as well. Following these mandates successfully is certainly more of a journey than a destination when working with youngsters who demonstrate severe and challenging behaviors.

While the information presented here is valid from a parent's point of view, this book specifically addresses the school's position and is meant to be a companion to the second edition of *Data Without Tears* (Johnston, 2014). The book is brief, to the point, and intended to reframe an educator's thinking about the purposes and function of behavior. The dirty little secret here is this: I want you to think about a kid's challenging behavior in such a way that, eventually, you will automatically implement strategies that will result in an immediate decrease in problems and know what to do to keep it that way. This book is NOT about meaningless paperwork. This book is about answering the age-old question "Why on earth does the kid do that?" quickly and effectively.

2

It's All in How You Look at It

Traditional Versus Preventative Approaches to Behavior Change

What's Typical

Face it: The time-honored way to get kids to stop "misbehaving" is to punish them (or give them *consequences,* a term typically used synonymously with *punishment,* though it means something very different). Even the most enlightened institutions and parents use this reactive approach to solving problems: Wait for a crisis to occur and then address the problem.

Frankly, this approach works for many kids. But what about those who are unaffected by what we consider to be punishment? Between one and five percent of any student body do not respond to traditional disciplinary measures (PBIS, 2014). They're the kids who are in the principal's office daily, who haven't had recess since 2006, and who are labeled by parents and teachers as a bad influence on the "good kids." They are the students who make teaching even harder than it is and who use up much of our available time and resources.

Reactive, crisis-driven strategies are what we educators use first to solve the behavior challenges presented by these few kids. When they don't work, when we have used up all our "tricks and treats," then what happens? Way too often, we blame the parents. We say things like "She comes from such a bad home, you know" or "That mom (or dad) lets her get away with this at home, so what can we expect to do in just six hours a day?" Or we blame the kid and/or the kid's diagnosis: "She has Tourette's, ADHD, autism, bipolar disorder"—just fill in the blank. Causal factors such as parental failure or "within-child" foci place the onus of responsibility squarely on someone else's shoulders and send a powerful message to kids and families. The message is this: "I, the teacher, can't handle you" or "You are much more powerful than I am, and therefore you must be sent somewhere far away from me."

My colleague Jim Jones puts it like this: Say you have a sick child, and you take her to the doctor. The doctor runs all sorts of tests, then brings the youngster back to you and says, "Mom and Dad, I've run all the tests I can run, and I can't find anything wrong with her. It must be something you're doing wrong at home." Wild analogy, right, but how often does this happen in the eduational realm? And the kicker is that many of the parents of these youth see US as the professionals and hope WE can give THEM some help.

I remind the teachers and administrators I work with that if traditional reactive strategies were going to solve their problem with a youngster, the problem would have been resolved by now. So let's approach the problems from a different direction.

The Simple A-B-Cs of Learning

A behaviorist explains learning and human behavior in terms of what comes before a behavior, *antecedents* (A), and what comes after the behavior, *consequences* (C). Any behavior, when followed by something that is liked or valued, will be "learned." In the future, a person is very likely to repeat the new behavior because he or she expects to experience the same positive outcome. If, however, the behavior is followed by an experience (consequence) that is not pleasant, chances are that the behavior will not be repeated.

Antecedents (A) are anything that triggers a behavior to occur. They include events, situations, contexts, environments, and even internal feelings and thoughts. To reiterate, experiences that follow a behavior—such as treats, social interactions, changes in environments, and so on—are called consequences (C). So this becomes the A-B-Cs of learning, also known as the A-B-C paradigm. Take a look at the example in Figure 1.

Let's analyze the interchange in this figure from the behaviorist's point of view. The first thing that happens in this short exchange is that Art says, "Good morning" to you. This is an antecedent (A). Although you may think that Art caused you to respond to him, that isn't really the case. Perhaps he did influence or trigger your response, but you could have responded in any number of different ways, such as saying, "What's so good about it?" or just ignoring him and walking away. Regardless, Art's greeting was an antecedent (A) to your saying, "Good morning." Your response (saying, "Good morning" to Art) is the *behavior* (B) in the ABC sequence.

What is the consequence (C)? What came immediately after your behavior or response to Art's greeting? In this case, he said, "It's good to see you today." This friendly comment (consequence) makes it more likely that you'll say good morning to Art tomorrow or the next day because he said something pleasant to you. Therefore, you have *learned* to say, "Good morning" to Art when you see him. Get it?

But what if you had ignored his greeting? In fact, what if you ignored his greeting for five days in a row? I'd bet that most people in this world would just stop saying good morning at all. In fact, if instead of ignoring him, you actually made a nasty comment, Art might never say good morning to you again, or he might even avoid coming within greeting distance altogether!

When we analyze the behavior of our students, we can't just focus on the behavior (B) alone. We need to look at all THREE variables, including antecedents (A), behaviors (B), and consequences (C). Antecedents are important because they occur before any problems are manifested. If you can change the antecedents and reduce the likelihood that a problem will occur, you are addressing problems proactively and preventing challenges.

FIGURE 1 A-B-C Example

Antecedent—Art sees you and says, "Good morning."

Behavior—You respond to him and say, "Good morning."

Consequence—Art then says, "It's good to see you today."

Traditional behavior management strategies look ONLY at consequences (C). This is not an efficient method of changing behavior, particularly when you're working with troubled kids. In fact, research indicates that using negative consequences alone to modify behavior is far less effective than applying antecedent preventative interventions in combination with consequence-based interventions (PBIS, 2014).

Founded on behavioral principles, positive behavior supports are a research- and evidence-based approach mandated in IDEA (see chapter 1) when developing behavior plans for students whose problems interfere with their learning or the learning of others. As educators, we are required to build plans that, by nature, are more proactive than reactive. In order to be proactive, however, we need to be able to predict the occurrence of a problem and "head it off at the pass," so to speak. And to do that, we must make an educated guess as to why the kid behaves in a maladaptive way. That, in a nutshell, means conducting an FBA.

The "Why" Versus the "How"

Once we analyze a cluster of challenging behaviors from the viewpoint of antecedents and consequences and hypothesize the "why," or purpose, of the behavior, we often find ourselves empathizing with the youngster. In other words, even though we may dislike the problem, the motivation for it can be very legitimate.

For example, a student may lack the academic skills that are expected of him. Devon is expected to complete math practice worksheets independently that are actually three grade levels above his instructional level! When faced with these demands, Devon tears up his assignments and runs out of the room. Carol, on the other hand, is nonverbal. Every time she enters the classroom, she runs to her teacher and hits her. She really loves her teacher; hitting is just Carol's idea of a good greeting. The "whys" can be perfectly understandable if you take into account the problems these students face. The way they behave, however, just isn't acceptable in the school context. After analyzing antecedents (A) and consequences (C), we begin to see that these problems don't just originate from "within-child" factors. Contextual and environmental factors contribute as well.

Before we go any further, let's be sure that we agree on some bottom-line assumptions regarding human behavior.

Assumption 1: All Behavior Has Purpose and Meaning

The definition of *behavior* is a person's action or a reaction in response to some type of external or internal stimuli. In other words, a person engages in a behavior for a specific reason, whether that reason is easily determined or not. From a behaviorist's perspective, there are only two possible explanations: The person wants to gain access to something, OR the person wants to avoid or escape something. That's it…one or the other. Take a look at Figure 2.

Assumption 2: All Behavior Communicates

This one is a no-brainer if you've accepted the first assumption. If there is a purpose to a behavior, then the behavior is designed to tell others what you want or don't want. All behavior has a communicative intent, regardless of its form. These messages are the "why," or function, of the behavior. Behavior may be saying, "I'm tired," "I'm bored," "I need help," and so on. Kids don't always realize the messages they are sending us. Their reactions and needs drive their behaviors, even if they have no real understanding of "why."

It is not, however, enough to say that the function or purpose of a youngster's behavior is to communicate. Too many times, I have sat in meetings with speech

FIGURE 2 **Functions of Behavior**

Gain access	Avoid or escape
Power/control over a person or situation	Academic demands
Peer or adult interactions	Peer or adult interactions
Attention from others	Attention from others
Activities or tangible items	Activities
Sensory stimulation	Sensory stimulation

therapists and other adults who stop here, particularly when the child is basically nonverbal. An FBA also must seek to answer WHAT the child is trying to say. Again, all behavior communicates something. It's that "something" that we need to delve into more deeply.

Assumption 3: Behavior Does Not Occur in a Vacuum

If all behavior has purpose, then it can't be random. Behavior often occurs in response to an environment or in order to control aspects of a situation. In other words, the CONTEXT actually affects the occurrence or nonoccurrence of a behavior.

Here's a silly example I always use in my lectures to get this point across: "Well, everyone, just call me observant, but I've noticed that today, none of you has come to this meeting…NAKED!" (Laugh, laugh, titter, titter.) "Why is that?" At this point, some wise guy thinks he or she is oh so clever and says something like "Because it's cold!" LOL! That's always the first statement, regardless of whether it's January or August. Then others will add things like "It wouldn't be pretty" and "I'd lose my job." Finally, someone will say, "It's not socially appropriate." "Okay," I say, "but I'll bet for all of you there IS some time in your life (I need NO details, thank you) when being naked IS socially appropriate." (Laugh, laugh, titter, titter.) I go on to explain that that's what I mean when I say that a behavior is affected by context: You might do one thing in the environment or context of your home and another in the environment or context of work.

Assumption 4: A Behavior Can Serve a Different Purpose Depending on the Context

This, too, is a no-brainer if you accept the other assumptions. Simply put, a behavior can be demonstrated for one purpose in, shall we say, the classroom and for another purpose, for example, in the gym. Rita is a great example of this. She starts yelling at the teacher as soon as she is given work to do. The teacher then sends Rita to the office, giving her exactly what she wants: escape from the demand. In the gym, Rita yells to cheer her teammates on during a game—same behavior, different functions. If we look at the behavior of "yelling" out of context, we won't be able to figure out the function.

Contemporary, Proactive Approaches to Eliminating Behavior Problems

In a proactive approach, we are as much or perhaps even more interested in what comes BEFORE a problem behavior occurs (antecedents, A) as what comes AFTER (consequences, C) when we are designing effective behavior plans. These are proactive and reactive strategies, respectively. Different from reactive strategies, positive behavior support, or PBS, relies heavily on proactive or antecedent strategies, which prevent problems from occurring altogether.

A second difference with a PBS approach is that we begin by assessing the function or the purpose of the behavior and use that information to design effective behavior plans. This is often the only successful way to work with really difficult kids. Punishment hasn't worked in the past, so why do we keep pinning our hopes of change on increasingly more punitive consequences? (A group of eighth-grade teachers once asked my advice on how to make their punishments hurt more!) In truth, we can't punish enough to make it worthwhile for all students to do what we want when we want it—it would be illegal!

When we begin to shift our way of looking at behavior problems, we don't discount things that may be going on with a youngster or with the youngster's family, but we do focus on the educational setting specifically. We look for the antecedents

(A) or triggers that precede the behavior (B). By the way, I can just hear some of you shouting at me, "But there AREN'T any antecedents!" If I only had a dollar for each time I've heard that, I'd be living in a villa in Tuscany. I'll talk more about this later, but for now just know that there are ALWAYS antecedents to behavior.

We can't control who the child is and where he or she comes from. This lack of control often becomes a source of an educator's frustration and hopelessness. But we CAN control environments and other triggers, and quite often this can be enough to change the life of a child in miraculous ways.

Using the FBA process, once a problem is identified we can hypothesize what the motivation is and why the kid chooses to behave in a certain way (and I use the word *choose* very loosely). Frequently, it comes down to this: The way a kid is attempting to meet a need is totally incongruent with the culture and context of the school setting. With a good FBA, it is possible to develop a behavior plan that works to help that kid meet that need in a more acceptable way.

What It Is and What It Ain't

Components of a Functional Behavior Assessment

An FBA is NOT a Form!

I know that the only thing educators like better than cool stickers, gadgets, and teacher toys are forms; we LOVE forms because we mistakenly believe that they make our lives easier and our jobs more controllable. Do me a favor and pick up almost any of those 1,012 FBA books I mentioned in chapter 1 or check out your school district's or your state's FBA rules and regulations. Look at all the forms and documents that honor our insatiable desire for checklists and fill-in-the-blanks. How do you feel about the FBA/BIP process now? Overwhelmed? Frantic? Are you ready to contact a career counselor? You can get lost in the notion that you have to complete each blank or you have failed in some way. Don't get me wrong; some forms are great if you know what you're doing and why. But, folks, I've got bad news for you: The form is not the FBA!

An FBA is a way of seeing and perceiving the behavior problem from many different angles; it allows you to understand the motivation behind the behavior problem even when the kid doesn't know it. I'm going to say this again to be sure you get it: The FORM is not the FBA. What a good form can do is direct your thinking in order to meet the main objective—answering the age-old question "Why does the kid do that?" As I've said, IDEA does not tell you how to conduct an FBA. The law only says you must do it. There are no directions, formats, or mandates for consistent documentation.

Believe it or not, that's a good thing, not a bad thing. It means that you can simplify the process as much as possible as long as you come up with a functional hypothesis, or make an educated guess, about why a youngster demonstrates a particular problem behavior. The catch is that the educated guess must be based on data: REAL data, not C.R.A.P. (Can't Rely on Any Part of It) data.

What Does an FBA Tell Us?

When you ask the question "Why," you are asking about the function the behavior serves from the youngster's perspective. If you do this right, a functional assessment results in the following:

- First, a clear description of the problem behavior.
- Second, times, situations, and events that predict when the behavior will or will not occur.
- Finally, a hypothesis as to what is gained or avoided by the behavior.

The first item is often where things go terribly wrong in the process. When we look at a really troubled kid, he or she appears to have so many problems or challenging behaviors that it's difficult to choose one to focus on. Typically, everything the kid does wrong is dumped into the FBA because teachers are so frustrated and upset by the youngster's acting out.

Folks, it is IMPOSSIBLE to conduct a good FBA when there are 53 different behaviors listed as the problem. It is very important that the professionals working with the kid cluster all the problems into discrete actions or events and then PRIORITIZE to determine which need to address first.

The second item refers to the antecedents to behavior problems. There are several types of antecedents: people, settings, environmental triggers, and so on. Once again, if I had a dollar for every teacher who told me "There are no antecedents" to a student's problem behavior, I'd not only live in Tuscany, but I'd be richer than Oprah! There are ALWAYS antecedents and triggers; identifying them can be tricky, however.

The last item, although there are only two choices, can be difficult for teachers, too. Teachers sometimes think too much and get lost in the weeds trying to follow the information they have. They find it very difficult to stay objective when analyzing the data. If you get it wrong here, you'll be designing a BIP that won't work. The problem behavior may even increase. The *consequences,* and I use the term from a behaviorist's perspective, that we are most concerned with in this process are the reactions and payoffs that the kid gets IMMEDIATELY after demonstrating the behavior. (Not that there aren't long-term consequences that affect the reoccurrence of problems.)

These three components can take days and weeks to discover when a student is complicated and there is much material to review. In most cases, however, the function is so obvious that the process can take just minutes. That's IF the team follows a structured, step-by-step, methodical line of thinking. Let's take a look at some no-brainers first.

Derek Has a Knife!

Does this situation sound familiar? You've got a kid, Derek, on an IEP due to a mild/moderate cognitive disability. He hasn't had any behavior problems in the past. He's a nice kid from a nice family. He does have some trouble making friends. The next thing you know, you find out from another student that Derek has a Swiss

Army knife that he's been showing to his peers all day. Apparently, he received the knife as a gift the night before.

There is NO choice in this situation. The school has a very clear zero-tolerance policy when it comes to weapons. It means expulsion. Since Derek hasn't had a problem before, there is no BIP to review and modify. Therefore, an FBA and a BIP "must be committed to writing as documentary evidence that the school is in compliance with IDEA."

This is a situation that will take only minutes. Let me show you:

1. Behavior of concern: Derek brought a weapon (i.e., Swiss Army knife) to school.

2. Identification of times, situations, and events that predict when the behavior will or will not occur: Showing his friends during unsupervised times of the school day.

3. Identification of what is gained or avoided by the behavior: Gaining attention and admiration from peers.

The school's consequence for this behavior is expulsion. Since Derek is on an IEP, the school district will provide some type of home instruction. A behavior plan focusing on social skills development would be appropriate. Since the law requires that FBAs and BIPs be committed to writing, Derek's might look like this.

DEREK'S FUNCTIONAL ASSESSMENT AND BEHAVIOR INTERVENTION PLAN

Problem behavior: Bringing a weapon to school

Functional hypothesis: Derek brought the weapon to school in order to GAIN ACCESS to peer attention and admiration.

Intervention strategies

- Direct instruction in social skills (e.g., how to make friends, making good decisions, etc.)

- Review of school rules and policies

- Completion of designated consequence per school district policy

- Contract with administrators regarding compliance with school policies once Derek returns to the school building

This isn't rocket science. In Derek's case, you need to follow the letter of the law, but it is unlikely he will repeat this behavior in the future. Although this is an unfortunate situation, Derek's FBA and BIP are pretty straightforward.

Here's another example: same behavior, very different story.

Jason Has a Knife!

Jason is on an IEP (severe learning disability), too, but he's had some problems with peers lately. Specifically, Jason has complained that a group of boys have been physically intimidating him. On this day, Jason brings a steak knife to school in his backpack. He sees the group of boys walking down the hallway, and he pulls the knife out of his bag and threatens them with it. A teacher witnesses this and calls the principal, who calls the police, and Jason is now up for expulsion. Although the behavior is identical, the FBA is different, as the following example shows.

Jason's Functional Assessment and Behavior Intervention Plan

Problem behavior: Bringing a weapon to school

Functional hypothesis: Jason brought the weapon to school in order to GAIN ACCESS to power and control over a group of boys who have been tormenting him.

Intervention strategies

- Review of school rules and policies

- Direct instruction, using the district's anti-bullying curriculum

- Completion of designated consequence per school district policy

- Since the incident was reported to the police, involvement of juvenile court

Jason and Derek demonstrate the same serious behavior. Both motivations are to GAIN ACCESS to something, but that something is very different. Derek did something stupid that is not likely to occur again, especially with parental support. Jason, on the other hand, has been the target of bullying many times, and some schoolwide interventions need to be put in place in addition to working with Jason individually.

Okay, one more time: Larry brings a knife to school, but his motivation is different from Derek's and Jason's.

Larry Has a Knife!

Larry is new to the school and comes with an IEP with the designated disability of severe emotional disturbance. Records indicate that he is frequently late or absent from class. Other problem behaviors include minor physical altercations, class disruptions, and disrespectful interactions that, in his other school, resulted in his being sent home or suspended. Academically, Larry scores several grade levels behind his peers in all areas.

Larry's former IEP team conducted an FBA. The hypothesis was that he engages in all these behavior problems to escape or avoid school (duh!). So the behavior plan says, among other interventions, that regardless of Larry's behavior he should not be sent home.

After two months of extremely challenging behavior on Larry's part, data from the former school setting and the new school setting indicate that Larry's very disruptive and aggressive behavior occurs several times a day. Because of the behavior plan in place, he is never sent home.

Larry has decided that the situation calls for desperate measures. Knowing perfectly well what will happen, he brings a knife to school. The team has no choice: expulsion. Unfortunately, the consequence is exactly what Larry is looking for. The following modification of the existing FBA/BIP, after review, can be written very quickly.

LARRY'S FUNCTIONAL ASSESSMENT AND BEHAVIOR INTERVENTION PLAN

Problem behavior: Bringing a weapon to school

Functional hypothesis: Larry brought the weapon to school in order to ESCAPE/AVOID school by being expelled.

Intervention strategies

- Recommendation for a small group for social skills instruction
- Consideration of an alternative setting designed specifically for youngsters with emotional/behavioral difficulties
- Adjustment of academic demands, using high interest–low ability materials

To sum up, Derek, Jason, and Larry demonstrate the same behavior for different reasons. Luckily, these reasons or functions are relatively easy to see. The behavior itself is also easy to identify. It is observable and measurable. Since a zero-tolerance policy with regard to weapons exists, little more assessment is needed.

In each of the cases presented, the information is clear and uncomplicated. Other examples of no-brainers include times kids bring drugs or alcohol to school or are consistently truant. So as you can see, FBAs don't always have to be an ordeal. They can be brief and take next to no time at all.

4

Eeeny, Meeny, Miney, Moe

Choosing and Describing the Target Behavior

Three Components of Behavior Descriptions

For the most part, when a student presents a challenging behavior, it is something that the teacher wants to either eliminate altogether or decrease drastically. Identifying this *target behavior* (i.e., the behavior you want to change) is one of the hardest parts of the process, in my opinion. It is where most school teams get off track right from the beginning of the FBA process. The result is an abundance of frustration and the ultimate failure of the behavior plan. Here's why:

1. Teams want to throw everything, including the kitchen sink, into the problem description, resulting in an inability to measure the success or failure of the behavior plan.

2. Teams fail to describe the behavior in discrete, observable, and measurable terms, resulting in an inability to measure the success or failure of the behavior plan.

3. Teams include causal factors (e.g., "When given a direction, Johnny chooses not to follow it because…") in the description, which concludes with a false functional hypotheses and results in an inability to measure the success or failure of the behavior plan.

What's the common factor here? In each case, you have an inability to measure the results. That means you are unable to collect reliable D-A-T-A.

These days, we are obsessed with that four-letter word. Unlike members of other professions, we educators have relied on our observations and impressions of results rather than really learning how to quantify intervention results. Thanks to No Child Left Behind, IDEA, and Response to Intervention (RTI), that doesn't fly any more. We must measure progress consistently, and that measurement process MUST be reliable. The key to making this work for you, particularly if you are working with several challenging students at a time, is KISS: Keep it Simple, Sweetheart.

There may be a thousand little things about a student's performance that would be interesting to know, but capturing them in a reliable, quantifiable manner is impossible. On the other hand, you may think of a great way to document variables, but if you have too many things to record, it may take longer to fill out the data sheets than it does to instruct the youngster! No wonder teachers get frustrated and overwhelmed. This is critical: Collect data only on what is absolutely necessary. Otherwise, you will make yourself crazy.

There are three essential components of a measurable target behavior: Description (also known as *topography,* or the shape of a behavior), Start Time and Stop Time, and the Escalation/De-Escalation Cycle (also known as the *behavior course*). Failure to clarify any one of these components will result in limited success.

Since I know how much educators like forms, I have created worksheets to help you think about all of the behavior problems a youngster may bring to the table and prioritize those that are of most immediate concern (see Appendix A). I hope they help you. Remember, however, a worksheet is NOT the FBA! It is only a place to start so you can organize your thinking and the thinking of others.

Behavior Description: What You See Is What Everyone Should See

The description of the behavior must be crystal clear to all persons involved so that it can be measured reliably. Look back at the no-brainer examples in chapter 3. The behavior description in each is "bringing a weapon to school." That's pretty clear to me. The knife is either present or not present; there is no gray area here, no judgment call. The behavior infraction falls under the disciplinary rule about weapons, but the description of the actual behavior is possession of a knife.

Before you can answer "Why?" you have to identify "What?" This is the hard part, believe me. I spend hours and hours of my time helping teachers objectively define what the behavior is. By objectively, I mean this: describing the problem behavior in observable, measurable terms WITHOUT including judgments, external events, or data-absent speculations. The description needs to communicate to another person exactly what the behavior looks like, feels like, sounds like, and so on. Think about the behavior description as reporting the reaction of the five senses. The more objective you can be, the better.

Figure 3 shows a form you can use to indicate different concerns you may have about a youngster. You can then check off and number the first, second, and third problems as the highest priorities for intervention. These are labels only. In and of themselves, they are not discrete enough to count, but they do help you to begin to clarify a behavior you're concerned about.

Let me ask you something: As you look at all these problems, do any of them typically happen at the same time? For example, when Gabe is physically aggressive he spits and kicks and swears, too? He may not ALWAYS spit when he's having a problem, but when he spits, he is almost always kicking and screaming, too. (A blank version of this form appears in Appendix A.)

The good news is that we can define a target behavior broadly enough in some cases to include associated problems, too, knowing that if we eliminate one or two of them, we eliminate all of them. This cluster of behaviors is considered to be a "response class," meaning that if one occurs the others are very likely to occur and can be included in the target behavior. (For a detailed explanation of response class, please see Alberto & Troutman, 2012.)

FIGURE 3 Gabe's Behavior Concerns and Priorities Checklist

Student ___GABE_____ Date _____5/22_____

Problem behaviors			Priority
1. Absent frequently	Yes	No	
2. Aggressive	(Yes)	No	#1
3. Angry	(Yes)	No	
4. Bossy	Yes	No	
5. Bullies peers	Yes	No	
6. Defiant	Yes	No	
7. Disobedient	(Yes)	No	
8. Disruptive	(Yes)	No	
9. Disturbed	Yes	No	
10. Doesn't follow directions	(Yes)	No	
11. Emotionally high and low	(Yes)	No	
12. Forgetful	Yes	No	
13. Hyperactive	Yes	No	
14. Impulsive	Yes	No	
15. Laughs inappropriately	Yes	No	
16. Lazy	Yes	No	
17. Makes noises	Yes	No	
18. Off task	Yes	No	
19. Oppositional	(Yes)	No	
20. Out of area	Yes	No	
21. Out of seat	(Yes)	No	
22. Poor peer relations	(Yes)	No	
23. Screams/yells	(Yes)	No	
24. Spits	(Yes)	No	#3
25. Swears	(Yes)	No	#2
26. Talks out	(Yes)	No	
27. Tantrums/meltdowns	Yes	No	
28. Tardy frequently	Yes	No	
29.	Yes	No	
30.	Yes	No	

Where most of us go wrong is using a "label only" descriptor. For instance, you often see "tantrum" as common label for behavior. However, a tantrum LOOKS different depending on who's having it. Think about what two- or three-year-olds look like when having a tantrum. In some cases, they fall on the ground, scream, cry, and so forth. But what about a 15-year-old? We could still label a cluster of behaviors as a tantrum, but it is likely to look very different, right?

Teachers frequently include judgment statements and assume causal factors in their descriptions. I tell educators that if you think you really know the behavior is demonstrated in order to gain attention, you don't need to bother with the FBA! The FBA is conducted in order to answer the why. No need to go any further if you're already convinced. But if you are unable to develop an effective plan for a student, it is very possible that your beliefs are incorrect. Leave them out. They don't belong in the behavior description.

Figure 4 gives you examples of labels, judgments, and clear descriptive statements. Given each list, which one describes the behavior so specifically that you and three of your best friends would agree when it is and isn't occurring? That's what we're looking for: a very clear statement that describes an observable behavior. Please notice that I frequently use an "e.g." at the end of my descriptive statements. Giving examples really helps the team working with a student to understand and see in their minds exactly what the kid does that is so problematic. Examples also provide a clearer understanding of what "lazy" looks like in the student.

Let's consider the cases of Tommy and Clare. Tommy, a youngster with ADHD who is so full of energy that he's nicknamed "The Tasmanian Devil," is also quite aggressive when he gets angry with teachers and other students. Here's the description of Tommy's aggressive behavior:

Tommy's "aggression" is defined as running into other students or adults, pushing, head butting, biting, and kicking, often leaving marks and bruises.

FIGURE 4 Labels, Judgments, and Clear Descriptive Statements

Labels	Judgments	Clear descriptions of behavior
Disruptive	When he doesn't get his way, he bothers others.	He leaves assigned area, runs around the classroom, bothers other students (e.g., pats them on the head, calls them names, etc.).
Off task	She stays up late each night and then sleeps in class.	She puts her head down on the desk for 30 seconds or more and remains in that position, not responding to adult cues.
Physical aggression	If another student teases him, he'll kick or hit.	He kicks or punches with a closed fist with such force as to leave marks and cause pain to another.
Disrespectful	When the teacher corrects her, she'll roll her eyes and won't respond to any question or direction.	She crosses her arms on her chest, cocks her head to the side, and contorts her face while rolling her eyes.
Bullies peers	He gets his buddies together and picks on the little kids.	He prevents a younger or more vulnerable student from walking in the hallway, pushes the student up against the lockers, may make demands that a student give him money, threatens the youngster by placing a closed fist near the youngster's eye, and otherwise intimidates the student to such a degree that the student won't look at him, tries to avoid walking in the same hallway, or otherwise indicates to a teacher the he or she is afraid.
Lies/cheats/steals	She always lies, and you can never trust her.	Makes declarations and statements that are later found to be untrue, claims other's work to be her own, takes others' property.
Excessive tardiness and absences	He fools around in the hallway and is late almost all the time.	He reports to class five minutes or more after the class begins.
Inappropriate language	He swears without even thinking about it. He obviously learned this from those parents!	He makes profane or vulgar statements (e.g., f___ you, sh___, g___ d___ it, etc.).

28

Clare, a young woman with severe limitations due to problems associated with autism, looks very different when she is aggressive. Here's that description:

Clare's "aggression" is defined as slapping a teacher with an open hand, rarely leaving a mark.

Now let's suppose you're a new substitute teacher. You have a choice of assignments for a one-week period: Tommy's classroom or Clare's. Which do you choose? Unless you are pretty masochistic, probably Clare's because you don't see as much of a threat in there. That's what a good behavioral description does for you and everyone else on the team. Because you can picture the behavior in your head, you know exactly what to expect. Since our experiences are vastly different, we are bound to have very different expectations as to what a problem actually is if it's described only in a general way. Just using the label "aggression" doesn't do us any good.

Start and Stop Time

For a behavior to be truly observable and measurable, it needs to be divided into discrete events. Think of it this way: It's easy to count pieces of candy or balls or spoons or any other kind of objects because they have physical characteristics that make it easy to recognize where one begins and ends. Start and Stop Times enable you to know this about a behavior and to count it accurately.

Just as for the behavior description, Start and Stop Times are totally dependent on the characteristics of the student and his or her past behavioral incidents. For example, I know, as Tommy's teacher, that once he gets going (i.e., he makes physical contact with his target), he will continue to be aggressive (as defined previously) until an adult intervenes. If the situation isn't monitored and totally resolved, Tommy will get up and go after another student. So, in my experience as Tommy's teacher, I can't trust him not to be aggressive until he has calmed down enough to follow my directions and complete an activity I direct him to do. If he can do that for about 15 minutes, I no longer worry that he'll be aggressive again—at least until the next time.

How many times do I count Tommy's behavior as having occurred? Only once. Despite how many kicks, hits, or shoves he manages to inflict on his target, I consider the entire behavioral sequence as a single event. That's not to say he might not have another incident later on during the day, but I'm pretty confident that the trigger of this aggressive incident is no longer relevant. Please understand that 15 minutes isn't any kind of standard. I chose 15 minutes because, in my experience with Tommy, this is how long it takes for him to get back to normal. Another kid may only take five, or two, or none at all. It all depends on the youngster.

TOMMY'S BEHAVIOR DESCRIPTION WITH START AND STOP TIMES

Description: Tommy's "aggression" is defined as running into other students or adults, pushing, head butting, biting, and kicking, often leaving marks and bruises.

Start/Stop Time: Tommy's "aggression," as defined, starts when he makes physical contact with another person and stops when he is no longer considered to be "aggressive" AND is following teacher directions for 15 minutes.

Clare's Start Time is the same as Tommy's, but her Stop Time is different, as you can see.

CLARE'S BEHAVIOR DESCRIPTION WITH START AND STOP TIMES

Description: Clare's "aggression" is defined as slapping a teacher with an open hand so lightly that there is rarely any pain or bruising.

Start/Stop Time: Clare's "aggression," as defined, starts when she has made physical contact with the teacher and stops when she removes her hand.

What's important here is to define the Start and Stop Time so the behavior becomes as discrete an event as possible. You can't count how many times something happens if you don't know when it begins and ends.

Escalation and De-Escalation Cycle: Thar She Blows!

The Escalation and De-escalation Cycle (also known as the *behavior course*) helps identify what the student looks like and how he or she behaves BEFORE and AF-TER the target behavior occurs. This information helps isolate behaviors as discrete events, which, in turn, allows you to count behaviors and keep data accurately. As is the case for the behavior description, the characteristics of an Escalation and De-escalation Cycle are different for every youngster.

Although I've said this before and will say it again, most plans to remediate challenging behaviors consist of reactive strategies alone. The PBS model requires us to provide proactive prevention strategies. The best way to prevent a behavior from occurring is to be able to predict when a behavior is likely to occur. One way to do that is to look at how the youngster's behavior spirals, or escalates, when he or she is upset.

After a behavior has been clearly described, we want to identify the *precursor behaviors,* or what happens (again in very observable, descriptive terms) just prior to the challenging behavior. By clearly identifying these levels for our students, we can avert trouble before it begins, which is ALWAYS better than letting students practice a problem behavior sequence over and over again. Understanding the ups and downs of behavior also helps us know when to intervene with corrective consequences, as we shall see.

Figures 5a and 5b show the Escalation and De-Escalation Cycle, respectively. Level 1 means everything is smooth sailing. However, we've all had the experience of knowing that trouble is brewing as soon as a kid walks into the classroom. It might be lack of eye contact, a frown, certain noises or comments, posture. We would consider that Level 2 behavior: Something is wrong, although the signs may be subtle. Typically, we also know when a problem will occur at any minute: That's what Level 3 is all about. Level 4 is the target behavior itself, as described in clear, measurable terms. This is the Start Time, when you begin collecting data.

FIGURE 5A Escalation Cycle

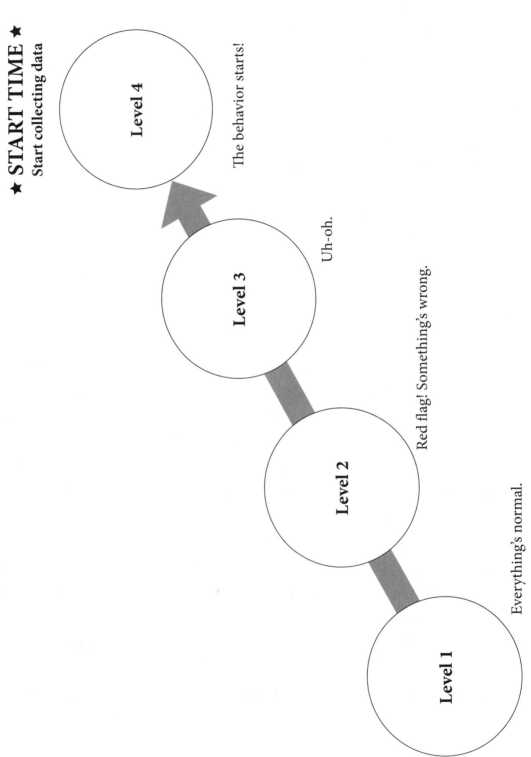

★ **START TIME** ★
Start collecting data

Level 4

The behavior starts!

Level 3

Uh-oh.

Level 2

Red flag! Something's wrong.

Level 1

Everything's normal.

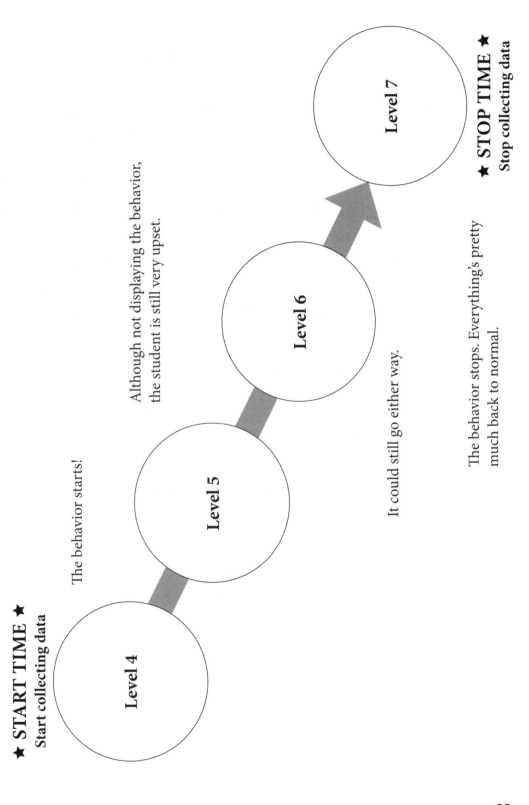

FIGURE 5B De-Escalation Cycle

★ START TIME ★
Start collecting data

The behavior starts!

Level 4

Level 5

Although not displaying the behavior, the student is still very upset.

Level 6

It could still go either way.

Level 7

★ STOP TIME ★
Stop collecting data

The behavior stops. Everything's pretty much back to normal.

33

As the youngster calms down, we can also identify the process or stages that occur. This De-Escalation Cycle begins with the target behavior (Level 4), as defined. Things are still iffy at Levels 5 and 6. You don't want to intervene too early, before the youngster is calm enough to hear the consequences of his or her actions and comply with the disciplinary follow-ups. If you intervene at Level 5 or 6, you could actually be throwing gasoline on the fire and inciting the kid to blow up all over again! Notice that Level 7 is pretty much the same as Level 1: The youngster is behaving normally (for him or her) and is ready to move on. This, folks, is the Stop Time.

Consider Tommy, "The Tasmanian Devil," again. He is always on the go, but you know the difference between his typical behavior and when he is getting frustrated or upset enough that you can predict a problem if you don't intervene. His Escalation Cycle looks like this.

TOMMY'S ESCALATION CYCLE

Level 1: Tommy is smiling, is very chatty with others, and can be easily redirected toward an activity with minimal teacher interactions.

Level 2: Tommy is not smiling; he makes comments about another student or group of students who are not treating him fairly.

Level 3: Tommy's face is contorted in an angry way. His eyes may be welling up with tears. He is pointing at other kids and accusing them of being cruel and unkind, calling him "stupid" or "dumb." He makes threatening comments, such as "I'm going to get you" or "You guys can't beat me up."

Level 4: The target behavior occurs: "aggression," defined as running into other students or adults, pushing, head butting, biting, and kicking, often leaving marks and bruises.

TOMMY'S DE-ESCALATION CYCLE

The De-Escalation Cycle includes Level 4 (the behavior starts) and continues as next described:

Level 4: The target behavior occurs: "aggression," defined as running into other students or adults, pushing, head butting, biting, and kicking, often leaving marks and bruises.

Level 5: The target behavior continues until adults intervene to break up the fight. Once separated, Tommy is placed in an isolated area, where he keeps his head down and won't make eye contact. If adults continue to speak to him, he'll say something like "Stop talking to me!" or make other angry noises or comments.

Level 6: Tommy raises his head, looks sad, complains about what the other kids said or did to him to make him mad, and continues to argue with adults if adults try to reason with him, give him commands, or describe consequences for his behavior.

Level 7: Tommy is compliant and follows all teacher directions for at least 15 minutes.

So, defining the target behavior involves three steps:

1. Describe the behavior in observable and measureable terms

2. Identify a Start and Stop Time.

3. Map out the Escalation and De-Escalation Cycle.

Once all three steps are completed, it's on to the dreaded data collection phase.

5

The Numbers Say It All

Data Collection

In the previous chapter, on defining the target behavior, we identified three steps. First describe the behavior in observable and measurable terms. Then clearly identify a Start and Stop Time so you can count each discrete behavioral event and collect data. Finally, map out the youngster's Escalation and De-Escalation Cycle so interventions can be devised to preempt the behavior or react to the behavior appropriately.

It's important to start taking data as soon as possible. Without data, you can make erroneous assumptions about cause and effect. Even though collecting data may or may not be the next step you'll take, this chapter will give you a brief overview of methods that are relatively easy. For more about how to take data, I refer you to *Data Without Tears* (Johnston, 2014).

How about an example? Greg, a good kid who can rival any politician when it comes to talking, has just about driven you and your colleagues crazy because you can't find anything that works to reduce his talking-out behavior. He disrupts not only his own learning but also the learning of his peers. In addition, you and other teachers lose concentration and instructional flow. Here is Greg's target behavior description.

GREG'S TALKING-OUT BEHAVIOR

Description: "Talking out"—During an instructional period, Greg verbalizes statements that may be on or off topic to peers or teacher without explicit permission from the teacher to speak and that can be heard one foot away.

Start/Stop Time: The behavior starts when any of the above description is present and ends when there has been no presence of the target behavior for 60 seconds or more.

Escalation and De-escalation Cycle

Level 1: During an instructional period, Greg is quiet and attending to the teacher.

Level 2: Greg begins to smile and giggle to himself softly.

Level 3: Greg appears to be excited, points to peers, and may show something on his paper to another and begin to talk or whisper to a peer.

Level 4: "Talking out"—During an instructional period, Greg verbalizes statements that may be on or off topic to peers or teacher without explicit permission from the teacher to speak and that can be heard one foot away. (Start Time)

Level 5: Greg may argue or say he wasn't talking.

Level 6: Greg mumbles to himself with his head bent, looking dejected.

Level 7: Greg is quiet and attending to the teacher for two minutes or more. (Stop Time)

Scatter Plot Data Collection

Most often, the data collection method of choice is frequency counting. Counting each time a behavior occurs is relatively easy as long as the target behavior occurs no more frequently than four or five times in an hour. A Scatter Plot Data Form can follow a student from teacher to teacher and class to class as well as serve to document frequency. Figure 6 shows a form for Greg. (A blank version of the form appears in Appendix A.)

1. In column one, "Class/activity/teachers" (e.g., math class, circle time, Mrs. Jones's class, etc.), document when and where the student is from the beginning to the end of each school day.

2. If the behavior occurs on any day during that activity, place a hash mark in the appropriate column and row.

3. Document any specific notes in the "Comments" column if you feel it is necessary to clarify details important to the situation.

4. Total the number of hash marks for each day in the "Total responses" row.

5. Compute an average for the day or week depending on what works in your setting, regardless of how many days your student actually attends. This way the data can be compared.

You can modify the form however it makes sense for your situation so that it becomes easy to use. If the form isn't easy, you'll end up with C.R.A.P. data, which can make or break your analysis and subsequent BIP. (I use a scatter plot method in chapter 7 to present Juan's case study.)

If the behavior occurs more frequently than four times an hour, you can still use the Scatter Plot Data Form, but instead of marking each instance, you can document whether the target behavior occurs any time during the class or activity. You use an *X* to indicate that the behavior occurred and an *O* to indicate when it doesn't. In this case, you calculate the number of class periods the behavior was demonstrated and average that over the week. Teachers tend not to like this method, however, because they feel recording the event only once per activity, regardless of how many times it occurs, underrepresents the problem. Also, using this method alone can cause difficulties when you are trying to demonstrate plan

FIGURE 6 Greg's Scatter Plot Data Form

Student __Greg__   Dates __2/10–2/14__

Record each occurrence of the target behavior with a hash mark by day and class/activity/teachers. Total the number of occurrences each day and calculate an average for the day or week.

Class/activity/teachers	Monday	Tuesday	Wednesday	Thursday	Friday	Comments
Literacy	//	/	0	/	//	Collect data only during instructional periods (see description).
Math	///	///	##	//	//	
Science	0	/	/	//	0	
Art/music	0	0	0	0	0	
Social science	##	/	## //	/	///	
Library/computer	0	0	0	0	0	
Total responses	10	6	13	6	7	Average incidents per ☑ day or ☐ week ___8.4___

effectiveness. That's because a student may reduce the number of incidents from ten to five per activity, but the data will remain the same.

If the behavior starts and never stops, or if the student is frequently removed from the room because of the behavior, a scatter plot isn't very helpful. You should look at using an interval or duration recording system.

Interval Data Collection

With a very high frequency behavior you may have to change your data collection method to an interval-recording format. Typically, you need an outside observer to take data this way because you can't teach and take data by yourself. You designate an observation period lasting anywhere from 10 to 15 minutes. Using a stopwatch or a clock with a second hand, you start observing the youngster at the beginning of the minute. If you see the target behavior ANY TIME during the interval, you put an *X* in the appropriate box. Once you've seen and recorded the behavior, you wait until the next interval begins and repeat the process: Observe and record for each designated interval. If you don't observe the behavior, you put an *O* in the box. I remind you that the target behavior AS DEFINED is what you're looking for.

Figure 7, Greg's Interval Data Form, shows data collected during Mrs. Carson's math class. A colleague of Mrs. Carson's takes interval data for 11 minutes and 20 seconds. That means he observes for a total of 63 intervals in all. Of those 63, Greg displays the target behavior in 23 of them. The results indicate that Greg was "talking out" 37 percent of the time during the observation period. (See Appendix A for a blank version of this form.)

When you collect interval data, the Stop Time from the behavior description is not relevant. If a behavior continues through several intervals, it is considered to be present and is therefore documented in each interval separately. You do not, however, record anything if you have observed precursor behavior, or behavior that is part of the Escalation and De-escalation Cycle before the Start Time. When

FIGURE 7 Greg's Interval Data Form

Name ___Greg___   Date ___2/11___

Mark an X in the box if the behavior occurs ANY TIME during that period. Mark an O if it does not.

Seconds

	10	20	30	40	50	60
1	O	O	X	X	X	X
2	X	X	X	O	O	O
3	O	O	O	X	X	X
4	X	X	X	O	O	O
5	X	X	X	X	X	O
6	O	O	O	O	O	O
7	O	O	O	O	O	O
8	O	O	X	X	X	X
9	X	O	O	O	O	O
10	O	O	O	O	O	O
11	O	O	O			
12						
13						
14						
15						
TOTAL Xs	4	3	5	4	4	3

Minutes

Number of intervals behavior was observed (i.e., Xs): ___23___

Number of intervals in total observation period: ___63___

Rate of behavior (Xs / total no. of intervals observed) = ___.365, or 37%___

42

you have completed your observations, you take the total number of intervals you observed the target behavior (i.e., *X*s) and divide this number by the total number of intervals in the observation period. This gives you the rate of behavior.

When using an interval-recording system, you want to be sure to collect samples across days and time of day or contexts. If the data are pretty similar across different situations, you can just report an average of all. If they are not, these differences will give you some clues as to triggers and reactions that you'll be taking a look at in the next chapter. Also, you'll know when to allocate additional resources for a successful BIP.

Time-Sampling Data Collection

If you aren't able to get someone else to observe and collect data, you can try using a time-sampling method. This is similar to the interval recording method, but instead of seconds, the intervals can be much larger: 5, 10, or even 15 minutes. The real difference here is that you document the behavior only if it occurs at the END of the interval, not during. By setting a timer or some other device that reminds you to look at your student right at that moment, you can get an estimate, however broad it might be, as to the frequency and pervasiveness of the behavior problem. Figure 8 shows a Time-Sampling Data Recording Form for Greg. (A blank version is provided in Appendix A.)

Teachers don't like method very much either because it also is a gross representation of the overall problem. See what Greg's data look like when taken as a time sample versus an interval sample? Regardless, remember that accurate data are better than C.R.A.P. data and that time sampling may be better than nothing.

FIGURE 8 Greg's Time-Sampling Data Form

Student ____Greg_____ Date __2/12_____

Mark an X in the box if the behavior occurs ANY TIME during that period. Mark an O if it does not.

Minutes

	10	20	30	40	50	60
1	X	O	X	X	O	X
2	O	O	X	X	X	O
3	O	X	O	O	O	O
TOTAL Xs	1	1	2	2	1	1

Number of intervals behavior was observed (i.e., Xs): _____8_____

Number of intervals in total observation period: _____18_____

Rate of behavior (Xs / total no. of intervals observed) = __.44, or 44%__

44

6

The Devil in the Details

Analyzing Antecedents and Consequences

It's time to take a closer look at antecedents (what comes before the target behavior) and consequences (what comes after) so that we can begin to think about the when, where, and why of problems.

In determining antecedents, your job is to spot social, classroom, and physical circumstances and environmental conditions that can set off the student's problem behavior. These may include things like medications taken or missed, illness or allergies, problematic sleep patterns, arguments with parents, confrontations, academic failure, poor eating routines, problems relating to transportation, negative social interactions with peers or adults, reprimands or corrections from teachers, boring tasks, structured or unstructured activities, extended work without a break, social isolation, and so on and so forth. These types of antecedents are also known as *setting events* or *triggers*. You'll begin to see that if you can predict a behavior, you can prevent it by changing settings or eliminating triggers.

While antecedents tell us when and where the behavior is likely to occur, consequences begin to tell us why. By understanding consequences (also known as the *maintaining consequences* or the *results)*, we begin to develop an understanding of the youngster and what needs are being met when he or she engages in problem behaviors. Understanding these consequences is essential if you want to change behavior.

The checklist for Carrie, shown in Figure 9, gives teachers a way to organize their thoughts about what could be happening in a problem situation. The left side is all about antecedents. It's difficult to think about these things in the heat of the moment, but considering patterns over time can be extremely helpful. Any of the items listed could precede any precursor behaviors that you have already identified as part of the Escalation and De-escalation Cycle. Some of these antecedents you may have knowledge of, and some you may not. It's all about detective work at this point.

When we pinpoint antecedents and consequences, we begin to develop an understanding of the youngster and what needs are being met by engaging in the problem behaviors. Take Carrie, for instance.

CARRIE'S ANTECEDENT, BEHAVIOR, AND CONSEQUENCES

Antecedent: Carrie gets teased by a peer.

Behavior: Carrie punches the peer with a closed fist one time.

Consequences: Carrie is sent to the office (immediate consequence); Carrie's parents are called (secondary consequence).

Data tell us that Carrie punches a peer on the average of one time per week. Each time, her parents are called. But she continues to punch peers when she's teased, so the "punishment" of calling home isn't really working, is it? Okay, okay... I can hear you out there: "If the parents would only punish Carrie at home when they were called, this wouldn't be a problem anymore!" You may be right, but even their punishment may not be enough to change this behavior if Carrie's main goal is to get sent to the office in the first place!

Being sent to the office doesn't seem to have any impact on Carrie's behavior either. Ask yourself, is there something about this consequence that could be attractive to Carrie? Maybe she's just happy to get away from the teasing. Or is it possible that Carrie engages in punching in order to exert power and control (an internal feeling) over the peer, which is an even stronger consequence than being

FIGURE 9 Carrie's Antecedents and Consequences Checklist

Student___*Carrie*_____Date___10/24_____

Use the back of this sheet to document any other triggers or consequences not listed.

Setting Events and Behavior Triggers		Immediate Consequences	
1. Academic demands/activities		1. Allowed access to preferred activity	
2. Academic failure		2. Assigment modified	
3. Allergies		3. Attention from adult	
4. Asked to wait		4. Attention from peers	
5. Conflicts at home		5. Given a break	
6. Conflicts at lunch time	√	6. Ignored by adults	
7. Conflicts during recess	√	7. Ignored by peers	
8. Conflicts in the hallway	√	8. Loss of privileges	
9. Conflicts on the bus		9. Moved to another area in classroom	
10. Correction received from adults		10. Peer support provided	
11. Difficult tasks		11. Personal time-out	
12. Easy tasks		12. Physical prompting	
13. Given multiple directions at one time		13. Provided physical reminders	
14. Hunger		14. Reaction from others	
15. Ignored		15. Reinforcement removed	
16. Illness		16. Seat changed	
17. Isolation from peers		17. Sent to hallway	
18. Long tasks		18. Sent to in-school support	
19. Missed/changed medication		19. Sent to office	√
20. Negative peers	√	20. Sent to resource room	
21. Pain		21. Time-out given	
22. Physical effort		22. Takes a walk	
23. Preferred activities taken away			
24. Sensory overload			
25. Sleep problems			
26. Transitions		Secondary Consequences	
27. Working without a break		1. Expulsion	
28. Working with a peer		2. Out-of-school suspension	
29. Working independently		3. In-school suspension	
30. Working in a small group	√	4. Detention	
31. Working in a large group		5. Parent contacted	√
32. Working away from desk		6. None	

sent to the office or any punishment you might think of? As I've said, it's all about detective work.

Clearly and objectively assessing the immediate and secondary consequences of a kid's behavior is the second hardest thing to do in the FBA process, next to writing a measurable behavior description. That's because most of us have our own preconceived ideas about why things happen. Our judgments color our perceptions. Once again, if you already KNOW why a youngster engages in a behavior (e.g., he wants my attention, she doesn't like hearing "no," and so on) then why are you bothering with the process of functional behavioral analysis at all?

Look at the "Consequences" column in Figure 9. As we know, according to the behaviorist's point of view, all behavior is motivated by one of two things: desire to escape or avoid unpleasant circumstances OR desire to gain access to something. That doesn't mean that the same behavior, on the surface, can't be motivated by both types of consequences and reinforcement under different situations. That's why you conduct a detailed FBA: to understand the circumstances or contexts in which an individual seeks to gain access to something and the circumstances in which the behavior may be an effort to avoid something else. The devil is ALWAYS in the details, folks.

Sometimes, particularly when I'm working with younger students or youngsters who are developmentally challenged, I may ask the teachers to substitute an A-B-C Form I design especially for the situation. A typical A-B-C sheet is given out to teachers for them to record the details of a particular behavioral incident. These sheets just give columns headed "A," "B," and "C." Everything else is blank. The teacher is supposed to fill in what comes before, during, and after the behavior. My problem with this type of open-ended data sheet is that teachers are just too busy to record problem behaviors immediately. When they get around to it (if they get around to it), it is usually at the end of the day, and they are relying on their memories to record the details. Unfortunately, what results is generally C.R.A.P. data. My feeling is this: If it isn't good data, why take it? No teacher has the time to do this!

Once we have written and clarified the youngster's target behavior, it's possible to design a recording form that's easier to use and that generates much better data. Instead of writing notes, the teacher only needs to place check marks in the "Antecedent" column and the "Consequence" column. We'll see how the form can be customized for a particular youngster in the case study that follows.

Case Study: Jack Be Quick

One team I worked with was having significant difficulties with Jack, a first grader with problems associated with severe autism. When I first spoke to Jack's teacher, she described Jack's behavior as "extremely dangerous." She said that Jack targeted both teachers and students, leaving marks and bruises, and that the aggressive behavior occurred all day long and was unpredictable. Neither she nor her educational aides could see any antecedents to the problem (there's another dollar toward my Tuscan retreat!), and the youngster was equally problematic in his home.

To get the bigger picture, it's important for you to know that Jack was totally nonverbal at this time. He had the ability to connect with people briefly but more often preferred to retreat into his own world, like many severely autistic children. He often twirled around, jumping up and down while quickly shaking his head from side to side. This self-stimulating behavior was often difficult to interrupt. Finally, finding ways to reinforce Jack to encourage participation in preacademic activities was also a challenge. By the time I was called in to assist the team, Jack was no longer allowed to be anywhere near a peer, and all his instruction was carried out in a one-to-one setting. The teachers wore arm protection to reduce the severity of their injuries. The day before my arrival, Jack had bitten an educational aide so badly that she had to be sent to the emergency room for stitches.

I asked to see the teacher's data, and it was all over the place. I really couldn't tell when, where, or with whom the problems occurred. In the teacher's defense, she and the assistants spent most of their time reacting to Jack's aggression and keeping the other kids safe. So we started with a clarification of the target behavior. After several tries, the teacher agreed on the following behavior description.

Jack's Aggressive Behavior

Description: "Physical aggression," defined as hitting, pinching, kicking, scratching, or biting another individual with such force as to cause pain or leave marks.

Start/Stop Time: "Physical aggression" starts when Jack engages in the above behavior with such force as to cause pain or leave marks and stops when Jack is engaged in a teacher-directed activity for five minutes or more.

Escalation and De-escalation Cycle

Level 1: Jack is smiling and humming to himself.

Level 2: Jack may show tension in his face; he may make grunting sounds or whine and often makes a moaning sound.

Level 3: Jack begins to cry, his eyes may get very round and appear fixed, his neck and jaw may become very tight and pronounced.

Level 4: "Physical aggression" defined as hitting, pinching, kicking, scratching, or biting another individual with such force as to cause pain or leave marks. (Start Time)

Level 5: Jack's face looks sad, and he is crying softly.

Level 6: Jack tries to stroke the peer or adult he hurt.

Level 7: Jack is engaged in an activity as directed by his teachers or his schedule for one minute or more. (Stop Time)

Remember, the teacher insisted that the behavior happened almost all day long. She couldn't think of a time when she could relax and be sure Jack wouldn't be aggressive. She had used a typical A-B-C chart, where she and her assistants made numerous notes and comments in the blank columns to document these problems.

I give her credit: There were dozens of these charts with different notations all over them. Unfortunately, I could tell that they were most likely filled out at the end of each grueling day of running after this young man. The teacher admitted that she and her aides would sit down after the kids left and talk about what happened with Jack throughout the day. Here's my problem with that: If I had to rely on my memory after a day like that, I wouldn't be able to remember any details! (Yes, I know I'm old and I can't remember what I did five minutes ago, but I couldn't have remembered all that at when I was 25 years young.) The result was C.R.A.P. data, at least as far as the close inspection of events that we needed in order to help this kid.

So, after observing Jack in his class and interviewing his teachers, I asked them to use the A-B-C Recording Form I created (see Figure 10). I explained that they should put the date in the first column, check off their observation of the antecedent to the behavior, indicate whether the aggression was directed toward an adult or peer, and check off the most IMMEDIATE consequence of the behavior. I also added a severity rating: 1 = low, 2 = medium, and 3 = high. As we shall see, sometimes this subjective rating scale can give a clearer picture about just how big the problem is in the teacher's eyes. The real key here was that this recording had to be made within five minutes of the behavior's occurrence.

I came back the next day and found that there were still some problems with the data system I provided. First, it was clear by what appeared in the "Comments" column that the teacher and her assistants were not recording "aggression" as defined. For instance, one of the comments said, "I got to him just before he touched Molly." This told me Jack had not made contact with Molly, nor did he direct his aggression toward the assistant. Nonetheless, the assistant had checked three antecedents: transition to new activity, received correction, and other (with the note). The teacher indicated that the incident was toward a peer and then checked two columns under "Consequences": redirected to activity and full physical prompt to comply. This was only one example. Read through the chart and see if you can find other interesting issues that the data sheet highlights.

FIGURE 10 Jack's First A-B-C Recording Form

Name ___Jack_____ Dates __3/10–3/12_____

Date	Antecedent							Behavior			Consequence									Comments
	Loud noises	Asked to wait	Transition to new activity	Academic or activity demand	Preferred activity interrupted	Received correction	Other (note)	Toward adult	Toward peer	Severity (0–3)	Redirected to activity	Ignored	Victim reacted (e.g., cried, yelled, etc.)	Others yelled/got upset	Given break	Given time away	Given tangible reinforcer	Full physical prompt to comply	Other (note)	
3/10			X															X		
3/10			X			X	X	X		3	X							X		Got to him before he hit Molly.
3/11			X			X		X		3	X	X				X		X		Kept kicking the table.
3/11			X			X		X		3						X		X		Tried to bite me.
3/12	X		X		X			X		3								X		Ran out of the room.
Totals	1	0	5	0	1	3	1	3	1		2	1	0	0	0	2	0	5	0	

We started over. I advised the teacher to check only one antecedent and one consequence, if at all possible. If the situation called for more detail, the teacher and her assistants were to use the "Other" category and note the issue under "Comments." And my most important point: Count the incident *only* if Jack engaged in the target behavior as defined—in other words, with such force as to cause pain or leave marks, as described in the behavior description.

As you can see in Figure 11, at my next visit, data recording was going better. The teacher checked only one antecedent and one consequence per occurrence, and the picture of Jack's aggression was becoming clearer. Over five days of data recording, the teacher recorded seven incidents. Of the seven, four occurred just after a transition from one activity to a next, two occurred when Jack was asked to wait, and one occurred when an activity Jack really liked was interrupted. All of the incidents were directed toward adults, and consequences included six "given a break" consequences and one full physical prompt. That physical contact resulted in a major injury—a bite wound. (That information is important to keep in mind when designing a behavior intervention plan.) Finally, if you noticed, each incident was rated as a "3" in severity, just as in the form from the week before. Because the teachers didn't see any differences in severity, even though they noted a major injury, it confirmed my suspicion that, while informative regarding the level of teacher anxiety, the severity data for the actual target behavior fell into the C.R.A.P. category.

I pointed out to the teacher that, although seven incidents were a lot, the behavior as defined wasn't occurring all the time, as she had thought. She did say that she and the assistants spent a great deal of time intervening before the aggression occurred in order to prevent it. That was a good thing, I told her, because prevention is important. Now it was time to use the data we had to help design more effective strategies that could extinguish Jack's aggressive behavior altogether.

Over the next several months, Jack made significant progress. Concerns about Jack's dangerous behaviors were pretty much gone within the first two weeks of

FIGURE 11 Jack's Second A-B-C Recording Form

Name ___Jack_____ Dates ___3/15–3/20___

Date	Loud noises	Asked to wait	Transition to new activity	Academic or activity demand	Preferred activity interrupted	Received correction	Other (note)	Toward adult	Toward peer	Severity (0–3)	Redirected to activity	Ignored	Victim reacted (e.g., cried, yelled, etc.)	Others yelled/got upset	Given break	Given time away	Given tangible reinforcer	Full physical prompt to comply	Other (note)	Comments
	Antecedent							Behavior			Consequence									
3/15			X					X		3					X					
3/17		X						X		3					X					
3/17		X						X		3					X					
3/18			X					X		3					X					
3/18			X					X		3					X					
3/19			X					X		3								X		Major injury: bite wound
3/20					X			X		3						X				
Totals	0	2	4	0	1	0	0	7	0		0	0	0	0	5	1	0	1	0	

implementing his behavior plan, and the teachers were able to introduce more functional academic activities and increase his expressive language by using a picture exchange communication model.

A blank version of the A-B-C Recording Form appears in Appendix A. I haven't included specific antecedents, behavior, and consequences. Your mileage may vary—in other words, each kid's situation will be different, and the form should reflect that. The next chapter discusses analyzing the contexts in which the behaviors occur.

Location, Location, Location

Analyzing Contexts

Remember the "naked" story I told in chapter 2? My audience and I talked about how attending a lecture without clothes on is probably not appropriate, yet not wearing clothes at other times could be very appropriate. (Once again, no details required here!) Analyzing contexts means giving very careful consideration to which situations or events predict or increase the likelihood that a youngster's target behavior will occur.

To show how to dig deeper into contexts, here's the story of Juan, a 10-year-old boy who made friends easily but was very impulsive and found it difficult to sit quietly during instruction or when he was expected to complete assignments. Figure 12 shows his baseline data, collected using a scatter plot format. Five days (one school week) of raw baseline data indicate that Juan was aggressive 14 times, or 2.8 times a day.

JUAN'S AGGRESSIVE BEHAVIOR

Description: "Physical aggression," defined as any of the following: karate movements; kicking, head butting, pushing, or otherwise making physical contact with others. Contact is rarely hurtful but is extremely disruptive to others.

FIGURE 12 Juan's Scatter Plot Data Form

Student _Juan_   Dates _9/8–9/12_

Record each occurrence of the target behavior with a hash mark by day and class/activity/teachers. Total the number of occurrences each day and calculate an average for the day or week.

Class/activity/teachers	Monday	Tuesday	Wednesday	Thursday	Friday	Comments
Homeroom, morning journal—Mrs. Rogers	0	0	0	0	0	
Language arts—Mrs. Rogers	1	1	1	1	1	
Specials: art, music, PE rotations	0	0	0	0	0	
Bathroom break and independent catch-up—Mrs. Rogers	0	0	0	0	0	
Math—Mr. Carter	0	1	1	0	1	
Lunch/recess	0	0	1	0	0	
Social studies—Mrs. Rogers	1	1	0	0	1	
Resource room (special ed)—Mrs. Kelly	1	0	0	0	0	
Science—Mr. Carter	0	0	1	0	0	
Dismissal—Mrs. Rogers	0	0	0	0	0	
Total responses	3	3	4	1	3	**Average incidents per ☑ day or ☐ week** _2.8_

58

Start/Stop Time: The behavior starts when Juan makes physical contact, as described. The behavior stops when Juan refrains from physical aggression and is engaged in a teacher-designated activity for 15 minutes or longer.

Escalation and De-escalation Cycle

Level 1: Juan is very compliant and follows the teacher's directions the first time they're given.

Level 2: Juan states that he refuses to continue working, and he may shove his book or materials off the desk onto the floor.

Level 3: Juan gets out of his seat, begins to yell and walk around the classroom, disrupting classmates.

Level 4: "Physical aggression," defined as any of the following: karate movements; kicking, head butting, pushing, or otherwise making physical contact with others. Contact is rarely hurtful but is extremely disruptive to others. (Start Time)

Level 5: After he is no longer making physical contact, Juan will lie on the floor under his desk and refuse to talk to an adult.

Level 6: Juan will go to his desk and put his head down but will respond to adults verbally.

Level 7: Juan will raise his head, make eye contact with an adult and follow simple one-step directions. (Stop Time)

Timeline Interview

One of the best ways I've found to take a closer look at school contexts is by conducting a timeline interview with the teacher describing each minute of the student's day. After the teacher describes what the student is doing at a specific point in time, I ask the teacher to consider how likely the behavior is to occur. This is a relatively simple procedure and is very informative. I ask the teacher to assign a number from zero to four, zero meaning the behavior NEVER occurs at that time and four meaning the behavior almost ALWAYS occurs then. Once the interview is completed, the team has a better idea of the extent of the problem and can begin to consider what resources are required and when and where they are needed most.

Here's the timeline interview I conducted with Mrs. Rogers, Juan's homeroom teacher. If it seems like I'm not saying much, you're right. I am, however, listening very closely.

Me: What time does Juan get to school?

Teacher: He comes about 8:30.

Me: Where is he?

Teacher: Homeroom.

Me: On a scale of zero to four, zero meaning it never happens and four meaning it happens daily, how likely is it that Juan will become aggressive at that time?

Teacher: It's rare, but he had a problem there on a couple of occasions. I'd say a one.

Me: Okay, what comes next?

Teacher: He stays with me for language arts.

Me: How likely is there to be a problem at that time?

Teacher: A four. I can't remember a day that he didn't start something.

Me: Okay, what comes next?

Teacher: Specials, either music, art, or gym.

Me: How would you rate that time, zero to four?

Teacher: A zero. He never has problems in any of those situations.

Me: Then what happens?

Teacher: We have a break. Kids are allowed to go to the restroom, they can do independent catch-up work, they can read a magazine—anything they want that doesn't involve a lot of talking or socializing. He doesn't have problems during this time at all. I'd give it a zero.

Me: Then what?

Teacher: Then he goes with the class to Mr. Carter for math. I'd say that would be about a two. Sometimes, sometimes not.

Me: Then what?

Teacher: Lunch and recess. There usually isn't a problem there, so I'd say a one.

Me: After lunch and recess, what comes next?

Teacher: He comes back to me for social studies, and I have a problem with him every day. Definitely a four.

Me: When you say a problem, do you mean he's aggressive, as described in our definition?

Teacher: Yes, definitely.

Me: Then what?

Teacher: He goes to Ms. Kelly, the special education teacher, to get help with his homework and other supports. He can have the same trouble with her but not all the time. I'd give it a two.

Me: Then what?

Teacher: The last class of the day is back with Mr. Carter for science. If they're doing a hands-on lab type of work, he's okay. Otherwise not. I'd say it would be a three.

Me: What happens at the end of the day?

Teacher: He comes back to me for dismissal. There is never an issue there, and he doesn't have problems getting to the bus either.

And so on. As you can see in Figure 13, the timeline gives us a good idea of where, when, and with whom problems are likely to occur. (A blank version of this form appears in Appendix A.) When you compare these impressions to the scatter plot data, many things become clearer. In Juan's case, you can see that he has problems during academic instruction. Right there, you have a critical piece of the puzzle when it comes to designing interventions to reduce the likelihood that Juan will demonstrate aggressive behaviors. We'll explore this further in later chapters.

FIGURE 13 Juan's School Context Analysis Form

Student ___Juan___   Date ___9/8___

Class/activity/teachers	0–Never	1–Rarely	2–Sometimes	3–Often	4–Always
Homeroom, morning journal—Mrs. Rogers		X			
Language arts—Mrs. Rogers					X
Specials: art, music, PE rotations	X				
Bathroom break and independent catch-up—Mrs. Rogers		X			
Math—Mr. Carter		X	X		
Lunch/recess		X			
Social studies—Mrs. Rogers					X
Resource room (special ed)—Mrs. Kelly			X		
Science—Mr. Carter				X	
Dismissal—Mrs. Rogers	X				

63

8

Why'd the Kid Do That?

Writing the Hypothesis Statement

I Repeat: What Does an FBA Tell Us?

The process of asking "why" leads us through a course of questions resulting in the following:

- A clear description of the problem behavior.

- Identification of times, situations, and events that predict when the behavior will or will not occur (antecedents/triggers).

- Identification of what is gained or avoided by the behavior (consequences/reactions).

Once you gather all this information, you need to organize and analyze it in order to form a hypothesis as to the reason a youngster continues to engage in the problem behavior despite all the efforts of adults to see that he or she does not. The reason the kid keeps doing whatever it is he or she is doing is often called the *maintaining consequence.*

The goal here is not to think too much: Just follow the logic of the information and ask yourself this: What is being gained by the behavior OR what is being avoided? In other words, what's the payoff? And when you're trying to understand the payoff, look first for the most immediate payoff. Often that's the key to making the change.

Writing the Hypothesis Statement

Write the hypothesis statement like this:

1. Who (the youngster in question)

2. The behavior (e.g., aggression, defiance, inappropriate language, etc.), as defined

3. The function (i.e., to gain access or toe escape/avoid)

4. What is to be gained or avoided (e.g., gain access to power and control, avoid academics, etc.)

Think back to Jack's case, in chapter 6. When we look at the antecedent data in Figure 11, it's pretty clear that transitions were a big problem for this little boy. Even being interrupted and being asked to wait meant that Jack's perception of "what comes next" was not jiving with what the teacher expected of him. Now consider the consequence data. It shows the teacher's use of a break or a full physical prompt so he will ultimately comply. Remember, the behavior was considered to be over (i.e., Stop Time) when "Jack is engaged in an activity as directed by his teachers or his schedule for one minute or more." This tells us that once Jack was directed, he was able to get back on track relatively quickly.

Here, then, is Jack's hypothesis statement:

Jack engages in "aggressive behavior," as defined, to AVOID transitioning to another activity.

Going back to Juan's case, in chapter 7, the data and context analysis revealed that Juan has problems during academic instruction. So, given this information, what's your hypothesis? Is Juan gaining access to attention, power, and control or something else? Or is he avoiding something, even for a little bit of time?

Although there are only two choices (what's gained or what's avoided), identifying maintaining consequences can be difficult. Teachers sometimes let what they believe to be true interfere with their ability to look at data objectively. They don't follow the logic of the information they have. But if you get it wrong here, you'll be designing a BIP that won't work. The behavior problem may even increase!

There are, of course, long-term consequences that affect the occurrence of problems, but when we're looking at kids, it is very likely that they are seeking the most immediate consequences, or the payoffs that happen right after the behavior. These immediate reactions are often determined by past history, experiences, belief systems, and so forth. For most situations, take the path of least resistance first. If that leads to a dead end or too much confusion, delve deeper.

A Million Dollar Question

A strategy I use when trying to assess antecedents and consequences is what I call the "Million Dollar Question." For me, it is the single most valuable piece of information I need in order to complete the assessment. I ask teachers this: "If I had very little time and I absolutely needed to see this kid demonstrate the problem behavior, what's the one thing you could do or say to guarantee that the problem will occur?" Ninety-five percent of the time, a teacher will say something like, "Oh, that's easy. Just _____." They'll fill in the blank with things like these:

- Tell him no.
- Announce a pop quiz.
- Let the class know when it's time for math.
- Ask her to correct a paper.
- Give another student a compliment.
- Ignore him.

Sometimes teachers are absolutely convinced that a youngster is behaving in a certain way to gain something. (I have found that 8 out of 10 teachers attribute "attention seeking" as the root of any identified problem behavior.) This question is a great way to see what the youngster really may be trying to escape.

The Functional Hypothesis Statement Form, included in Appendix A, can help you organize your thoughts. Figure 14 shows this form filled out for Juan. How does the information here align with your own hypothesis statement for this student?

FIGURE 14 Juan's Functional Hypothesis Statement Form

Student _____ *Juan* _____ Date _____ *9/13* _____

Target behavior: *Physical aggression* _____

Description: _*Karate movements; kicking, head butting, pushing,*_ _____

*or otherwise making physical contact with others* _____

Start Time: _____ *At time of contact* _____

_____

Stop Time: _____ *When no longer aggressive and engaged in teacher* ____

activity for 15 minutes or longer _____

1. What is the one event, demand, situation, person, etc. that will trigger the behavior IMMEDIATELY?

    *Any academic demand, particularly Mrs. Rogers' requests* _____

    *to complete independent work or reading* _____

2. Fill in the blanks.

    _____ *Juan* _____ (student's name) engages in

    *physical aggression* _____ (name the

    behavior) in order to GAIN ACCESS TO / ⟨ESCAPE OR AVOID⟩ (circle only one)

    *academic demands, particularly when asked* _____

    *to complete assignments independently and if reading* _____

    *is involved* _____ (name what and where).

9

It's Better to Be Bad Than Stupid

Teaching New Behavior

What Do We Know for Sure?

Do we ever know anything for sure? NO! But if you have walked through the FBA process that I've suggested, you know a good deal more than you did initially about the behavior in question, don't you? Here's what we've done so far:

1. We are in agreement that an FBA is not a form but a process.

2. We've gone through that process from an objective, behavioral perspective and defined the behavior in specific, observable, measurable terms as well as identified a Start and Stop Time so the target behavior is a discrete event and, therefore, can be measured accurately and reliably.

3. We have clarified a youngster's Escalation and De-Escalation Cycle, so we know when to intervene.

4. We can decide the most appropriate way to collect good data so that progress, or lack thereof, can be determined.

5. We know what events and contexts can trigger an occurrence of the problem.

6. We have agreed upon a hypothesis as to why a youngster is behaving inappropriately.

Believe me, I know that there is a great deal of information you may still want. For example, you may not have input from family members or professionals outside the school system who work with the student (e.g., physicians, therapists, etc.). Keep working on getting these folks to come to the table and provide their valuable input, but don't let this be a stumbling block for you. You should have enough valid and reliable information to begin the process of developing a plan and measuring its effects on the youngster's behavior problems. Remember: Keep taking data because it's the numbers that tell the story from now on.

Behavior Change Based on an Educative Philosophy

To create an effective plan, you really have to dig deep and identify what the youngster CAN do. Make a list of the things the kid does really well, even if it involves taking some less agreeable attributes and seeing them in a different, more positive way. See Figure 15 for some examples.

I think you get the picture. When it comes to designing strategies that will support positive behaviors and prevent inappropriate ones, you want to have every chance of engaging a youngster with a menu of reinforcement that he or she finds valuable and motivating. Spend time making this list, too. It will pay off in the end.

We now understand the purpose behind the problem behavior. It is the PURPOSE, or MOTIVATION, behind the behavior that becomes our focus when we are developing an effective behavior. The structure of the target behavior (i.e., what the behavior looks like) becomes somewhat irrelevant. What I mean is that we can no longer concentrate just on the inappropriate nature of the problem. We must design ways for the youngster to meet the need that drives that behavior. In fact, we hope that the intervention strategies will work so well that the original problem behavior becomes useless.

We are educators, so it is perfectly understandable that the foundation for this approach is teaching—teaching new, more acceptable alternative behaviors that

FIGURE 15 **Attribute Reversals**

Undesirable behavior	Strengths
Bullies younger students	Leader
Perseverates on one topic	Expert
Class clown	Entertainer
Off task, spending time drawing	Artist

will meet the same function as the target behavior does. There are two important caveats that must be taken in consideration if this approach has any chance of working for you:

1. When you seek to replace a behavior with a more acceptable alternative one, the new behavior must be EQUALLY EFFECTIVE.

2. When you seek to replace a behavior with a more acceptable alternative one, the new behavior must be EQUALLY EFFICIENT.

I'm making a big deal about this because these two points help to explain why many behavior plans are unsuccessful from the start. It's fine to say you want a kid to learn to raise his or her hand to get help rather than yelling and screaming. But frankly, it's easier to yell and scream. Here's a little insight into some of my own behavior problems that have yet to be eradicated.

For all the years I worked in a day treatment facility, I shared a secretary with several other lovely people. Regardless of who was doing what, across the board, I always got the secretary to do my work first. When I needed something and she was busy, I would stand by her desk and whine (in a cute sort of way). I would whine and whine and say please and make silly faces until she would laugh and relent and do my stuff. Inappropriate? Absolutely! Unfair? Very true, but it worked every time. It came to a point that other secretaries would ask me to whine to entertain them before they did many of the things I asked them to do!

So, in my trainings and workshops, when I tell this story I ask attendees to make suggestions to get rid of this insufferable behavior. Here are some of their typical responses:

- "Teach you to raise your hand."
- "Have the secretary ignore you."
- "Teach you to do the work yourself."
- "Give you a private secretary."

My favorite, of course, is the last one, which would never happen in a million years due to budget constraints. The others would never work either. First of all, if I raised my hand and the secretary didn't attend to me immediately, I would resort to whining. That suggestion just isn't EFFICIENT or EFFECTIVE enough for me. To get me to raise my hand, you would have to have a REALLY valuable reinforcer, like a private yacht or something. And once earned it, I'd most certainly revert back to easier behaviors. Get the picture? The second idea, get the secretary to ignore me, would be a nightmare for everyone. My behavior would escalate to such a level that the secretary would never be able to ignore me. I'm sure you've had kids like that. When you try to ignore their behavior (maybe by moving out of the area or looking away), they just get so loud that you can't ignore them anymore. Finally, it would take me forever to learn how to do what the secretary did for me, so that would be completely inefficient. And why, I ask you, would I ever be interested in working harder?

You can't expect a behavior plan to work if the foundation of the plan is weak. It is critical that the new skills identified to meet the same function be quick, easy, and effective for the student to accomplish. Thus you eliminate the need to demonstrate the challenging behavior altogether.

Skill Instruction: Teaching New Behavior

Throughout this book, we have been talking about alternative behaviors: What does a kid need to do INSTEAD of the problem behavior in order to get his or her needs met? What different behaviors can serve the same purpose as crying to escape peers, making noises to gain attention from the teacher, or fighting to gain power and control over the environment? When I was the director of a program for students with autism and significant behavioral challenges, "What do I need to teach?" was our mantra. Looking at the problem as a lack of skills really helped us see the problem in a different light.

SKILLS TO TEACH

Kids need to feel empowered. They need to feel that they have some control over their own environment and can make choices about what they do. Let's be honest, in a typical classroom, there really are very few choices to be made from the students' point of view: Draw the horse brown or black, do the odd or even problems, and so forth, but when kids feel they are stupid and that they can't do anything right, they either fight for their own identity (being bad) or give up (being stupid).

Remember, remember, remember: It is always better to be bad than stupid. You'll do anything to avoid letting peers and adults know you have absolutely no idea what's going on academically. If you feel stupid all the time, then you'll be darned if you'll let anybody know how stupid you are…right?

One of the first things we should take a look at is whether the academic program is right for the student. If it isn't, we need to fix it as best we can. So identifying specific academic skills that need to be addressed are always be part of developing an effective plan. When the function of a target behavior is escape/avoidance of the task, simply ask whether the task is too hard or too easy. I think more times than not, the task is too hard.

Other examples of general skills are self-help skills, vocational skills, and social skills. Every one of these areas should be looked at when analyzing a kid's problems. This is especially true when you have a youngster whose motivation, despite all your efforts, remains difficult for you to understand.

Purposeful skills are those that allow a youngster to complete a process or meet an expectation. Here are some purposeful skills that often need to be taught and practiced:

- Making choices

- Problem solving

- Following a schedule

- Predicting what comes next

- Organizing materials and time

One of the most critical skills humans need is a way to communicate their wants and needs. When verbal communication is unavailable to them, persons with significant disabilities are likely to resort to aggressive behaviors to tell teachers and caretakers that they don't feel well, want some attention, want a particular item, and so on. Talk about a purpose behind a behavior problem that is totally understandable and suitable! This is a great example of how the behavior demonstrated can be all wrong but the function is totally righteous. It's our job as teachers to give students a more functional way to communicate with the world.

COPING AND TOLERANCE SKILLS

Learning how to cope with situations we don't like and can't change is an important skill for all of us. Many of us have worked in stressful environments and found an easy way to cope: We quit! However, that's not always an option for us, and it's certainly not an option for students.

A word of caution here: As teachers, we expect our students to tolerate a great number of things they don't like. But if you look at the totality of what many students have, you can see their lives aren't very full of rewards. To ask a youngster who doesn't have very much fun in life to cope with and tolerate something negative will be much more difficult than asking a kid whose environment is rich with positive reinforcement and fun. So when you add coping and tolerance skill training to a kid's plan, be sure to include lots of fun that isn't contingent on anything the youngster needs to do—in other words, rewards that just happen and don't have to be earned.

Case Example: Keeping Carl Contained

Carl was a six-year-old boy whose behavior was disruptive, defined as a cluster of negative behaviors that occurred over a period of time, including one or more of the following: rolling on the floor, crawling around the classroom, hiding in small places, shouting out, and running in the classroom. Baseline data indicated that the target behavior, as defined, was occurring at a rate of 100 percent of time intervals observed in two 30-minute instructional periods while Carl was in the general education setting.

Prior to conducting a thorough FBA, the teachers stated that they thought Carl was engaging in disruptive behavior to gain the teacher's attention and the attention of his peers. Interestingly enough, however, the special education teacher reported that when he worked in a small group (fewer than four students) with the resource room teacher, he never displayed the behavior. The absence of the target behavior was confirmed by two additional 30-minute observations in the resource room.

After collecting the data, the team agreed on the following functional hypothesis:

Carl engages in "disruptive behavior" in order to escape and avoid academic instruction and independent tasks.

What caused the teachers to change their minds? If you guessed observation of different behavior in different settings, you're right. The general education teacher worked very hard to keep Carl on track. But the resource room teacher was not only able to keep Carl on track but also able to modify lessons and teaching strategies so he could understand what was going on and be academically successful. That's what we're talking about.

So now it's time to develop an effective behavior plan for Carl. And the first step is to ask yourself (let me hear you say it), "What am I going to teach?" What's the most obvious need Carl has? If you are thinking he needs to increase his academic skills in reading and math, you're right.

The resource room teacher is doing her best, and so is the general education teacher, but it's hard for Carl to generalize these newly learned skills to the general education setting. Generalizing skills isn't a foregone conclusion for many of these kids. More often than I'd like to admit, the only time these kids are getting access to appropriate instructional methods and academic modifications is in a resource setting, which often amounts to only 45 to 50 minutes per day. The rest of the day, academic accommodations consist of little more than extra time on a test, shortened assignments, or busywork, leading to boredom. This isn't always the case, but it happens too often to discount this situation as an anomaly.

Carl will need some additional heavy-duty strategies to make things work for him, but the first place to concentrate our efforts, for him and for many other kids, is on the academic skills and academic success.

The Grass Is Always Greener

Context Management

The Relationship of Context to Behavior

Teaching new skills takes time. So what can you do while you're waiting for the new skills to be learned and demonstrated? One of the first things is to change the youngster's environment or context. These changes are very often the most effective interventions.

Remember my "naked" story from chapter 2? Context is the ultimate antecedent. To be sure we're still on the same page here, I'll give you another example. Most of you would agree that yelling and screaming is not appropriate behavior in the classroom, right? But when is yelling and screaming okay? It would be more than appropriate in the gym during a relay race. If it were part of a play that the kids were acting in, it would be okay. However, in the school library, I can't think of a time that yelling and screaming would be tolerated. Context matters.

To give you another example, the rule "Raise your hand to speak" has to be context driven. It would be a good rule for group lessons, lining up to go in the hallway, and so on. But if you have kids in small groups working together, is it necessary for them to raise their hands before talking to each other? Is it necessary during lunchtime? No.

So context dictates rules and expectations for behavior, and setting events can either ignite or extinguish problems.

Physical Factors

Physical factors such as setting, lighting, noise level, and the number of people in a given space can have a real impact on how we behave. On a personal note, I don't like big parties. One of the biggest reasons is the number of people milling around. I'm the first one to knock into someone and spill my drink, then feel foolish and clumsy. When I absolutely have to go to a big party, my behavior in these situations tends to become rather silly and obnoxious, which generally works well to keep people at arm's length. In fact, it almost always earns me a spot on a couch in the corner by myself, which is okay by me.

Environmental issues are known to be problems for persons with severe disabilities. For example, many studies have been done on how fluorescent lighting effects learning and behavior in persons with autism (Bedell, 2013). So think carefully about those kids in your class who behave badly to reduce their discomfort in certain settings. Again, I claim it is better to be bad than stupid. (You can substitute any word for *stupid* here: *clumsy, boring, ugly,* etc.)

Years ago, I worked with a youngster who screamed every time we entered the gym or cafeteria. It didn't take rocket science to figure out that the noise level and the echoes were actually causing her pain. She was nonverbal and couldn't express her pain in any other way at the time. Our first strategy worked well. We gave her headphones with soft music playing. She was able to tolerate the lunchroom and gym and be with peers during these periods. Eventually, she actually got used to these environments and refused to wear the headphones at all. I think they interfered with her listening to the "girl talk" around the table. So a noisy environment set off the behavior. Giving her the headphones was a way to modify the context so she could tolerate it and eventually have more peer interactions, which she loved.

One of my mentors, Gary LaVigna, told me the story of a young man with problems associated with autism. The youngster (let's call him Brian) was in a high school multiple disabilities classroom and had been in the same district throughout his school career. Suddenly one January, Brian became aggressive. The teacher was mystified. Brian had never, ever demonstrated problem behaviors in the past. In fact, he was what they called a model student in their program. Dr. LaVigna was called in to see if he could help the situation because the student was in real danger of being placed in a more restrictive setting. Teachers told Dr. LaVigna that the behavior happened all day without any visible antecedents.

After interviewing Brian's teachers and observing Brian, Dr. LaVigna gathered the following facts:

1. "Aggression" meant hitting and kicking and scratching an adult (never a peer).

2. The Start Time was when an adult got within reach of Brian.

3. The Stop Time was when the adult moved out of reach of Brian.

4. The behavior occurred in first, third, and sixth periods only.

5. The behavior was most often directed toward the speech therapist; only one out of six incidents was directed toward the lead teacher. The speech therapist was in the room at the time.

After these brief observations, Dr. LaVigna had to ask about the speech therapist. What was going on there? Was she new to the job? No. Had she ever had problems with Brian before? No, in fact she had been working successfully with Brian for many years. Got a guess? "January" is a big clue here, folks.

The speech therapist had gotten a new perfume for Christmas, and she loved it. She loved it so much and had gotten so many compliments that she used it generously on herself. So generously, in fact, that Dr. LaVigna noticed it immediately himself. The bottom line was that it was a very pleasant smell to everyone but Brian. He was supersensitive to odors, and every time the speech therapist came near him, he had to communicate, "Get away from me," which he did in an aggressive manner. Once the speech therapist stopped using the perfume, Brian's aggressive behavior disappeared.

Talk about an easy fix, huh? Change the context, eliminate the behavior. But wait…what if Brian is walking in the mall with his family and smells that smell or any other smell that is noxious to him? We'd better teach him how to communicate or escape that odor in a more adaptive way, or he'll still be in trouble in the community.

By the way, Brian was aggressive one time with the teacher, too. Can you make a guess as to why? Yep, it was at the end of the day after the teacher and the speech therapist had a planning period together. The teacher commented on how much she liked the perfume, and sprayed some on herself. Brian let her know what he thought about that when she came back to the classroom that afternoon.

Interpersonal Factors

Contextually, how the group gets along is a significant factor in an individual student's behavior. The culture of the school in general and the atmosphere of the classroom itself are places to look for immediate context management.

Kids who enter a classroom where a teacher does not respect them or, even worse, ridicules them by using sarcasm and negative statements, are likely to give it back to that teacher in spades. That environment is the antithesis of what positive behavior supports are all about. We treat all kids and all adults with respect and dignity, always. Johnny Mercer and Harold Arlen said it best in the lyrics of the 1944 song "Accentuate the Positive." If you can follow this advice as a culture in your school, you'll reduce problems to a manageable number:

> You've got to accentuate the positive
> Eliminate the negative
> Latch on to the affirmative
> Don't mess with Mister In-Between.

So take a look at the interpersonal environment in which you expect your student to behave. If it is one that can't support the student, you may need to find a way to change it, even if such modifications are not typically made in your setting.

Expectations

Another critical area relating to context is expectations. Years and years of research studies indicate that teacher expectations impact student achievement both positively and negatively (e.g., Soragen, 2013; Stipek, 2002). Kids internalize what teachers think about them because teachers are in a position of authority over them. Time and time again, a youngster can achieve far more than test scores would predict if a teacher establishes high expectations and instills the confidence in a student that he or she is capable of meeting them.

Keeping expectations high for appropriate behavior is how kids can make the transition from a tightly structured alternative setting back into a general education setting. Sometimes it's the only way.

Curriculum Factors

There are many ways to adjust context in the area of program and curriculum. Giving kids choices is one way. These would be real choices, not just "You can do this math sheet or the other math sheet." Some REAL choices could include schedule arrangement. For example, we often have youngsters who have problems associated with autism or who are considered to be emotionally disturbed work through a daily "Premacked" schedule. David Premack famously observed that people will work through things they don't like to get to things they do (Premack & Premack, 1972). This means that we, the adults, pair activities that we are pretty sure the kid doesn't like so much but are necessary for him or her to meet academic benchmarks with activities we're pretty sure the kid will like, like computer time, breaks, and so on. Allowing a youngster to choose from a menu of "good stuff" to increase the chances that the not-so-fun stuff will get done gives the kid some control of what he or she does.

Many times, I've been called in to conduct an FBA and write a BIP for an older kid who is clearly in the wrong program. One in particular stands out. The youngster was a boy named Jordan who had struggled with reading throughout his school career. The district had provided tutor after tutor, specialized programs, and basically had turned themselves inside out to help this kid. At the time I met Jordan, he was at the end of his junior year in high school and was terrorizing the place. He loved band but was not allowed to participate because of his grades. He loved gym but had already earned his required credits in that area. He loved any and all parts of his school program that didn't involve reading. Miraculously, he was in line to graduate on time.

Now the absolute worst part of his day was Spanish. Jordan was at the bottom level and failing the course for the second time. His parents insisted that he take the language because, otherwise, he would not be able to get into a good college. The FBA took me about five minutes. My hypothesis was this:

Jordan engages in "disruptive behavior" (defined as leaving the assigned classroom, running up and down the hallways, planning and carrying out pranks, and otherwise disrupting the entire educational process) to avoid any task requiring reading and following directions.

Again, not rocket science. The only appropriate intervention in my opinion was to place Jordan in a vocational program immediately. When I asked him what he wanted to do after high school, he first said, "Go to college" but then told me that he really wanted to work for his uncle, who owned a business that sold agricultural machines. Jordan said the best part of working there was running all the machines and showing customers how to work them. Now, it's really important to know that as he described working for his uncle, his face was animated and his body language indicated his love of this work. He KNEW he was good at it. His uncle loved his help, too.

Asking his parents, of course, was a whole different story. They dreamed that he would go to college and maybe become a lawyer. Their reaction to my recommendation that Jordan's context and curriculum be changed significantly was not exactly positive. Even when we discussed the discrepancy between their vision for Jordan and his own, it was not an easy sell.

I tried to help Jordan's parents to see that his reading disability significantly interfered with most of his academic work, especially Spanish. Jordan had such a hard time reading English he couldn't even face trying to read and understand a foreign language. A final compromise was made: Jordan would attempt to pass Spanish one more time by taking it in summer school. Then, for his senior year, he would be enrolled in the vocational school. He would work in the mechanics program in the mornings and come back to the high school to take band and other electives in the afternoon. Credits would be adjusted fairly, according to his IEP, and he would graduate with his class.

Other Environmental Maneuvers

Other strategies that belong in the category of context change include ideas like providing a visual schedule, using a calculator, having a "safe place" to go to for a student who is super anxious, reducing the difficulty of tasks, reducing the amount of work, trying specific instructional methods, and so forth. The whole idea in making context changes is setting up different antecedents that will then trigger different, more appropriate behaviors. The consequence end of this paradigm is important, too. We want students to begin to experience reinforcement for these more appropriate behaviors so they are likely to be repeated in the future.

A Tale of Caution

Before I leave this chapter, I want to tell you about a very unfortunate case I was involved with many years ago. It shows how powerful context changes can be. However, if context management is not used in conjunction with teaching new skills, the ultimate results can have some serious side effects.

On the third day of a new school year, the school district's special education supervisor called me. She was frantic. Jarod, a young man who was considered to have high-functioning autism, was a new ninth-grade student at the high school. This high school had approximately 2,000 students. An experiment was being conducted that year to help younger students who might need more attention and academic support than others. A "pod" system was set up, and about 70 kids were assigned there. There were five teachers, representing all the curricular disciplines, who taught in a relatively self-contained area of the building. The students were able to change classes in a much less chaotic fashion than in the rest of the school, and the teachers met daily to discuss progress. A counselor was also assigned to this program. She taught life skills and other social skills. These students would be assigned to the pod for both ninth and tenth grade. This sounded like a perfect placement for Jarod, who was functioning at or above grade level in all areas.

Jarod did not fare well the first few days. In fact, he was running down the hallways of the other part of the building, literally bowling people over in his path. He was being taunted to the point that he became physically aggressive. The student body found this to be so entertaining that they would egg him on. These things all happened before he could step foot into his pod. In the pod, he was being disruptive and loud. Something had to be done—and quickly.

To make a very long story short, I met with the team and taught the FBA/BIP process. The hypothesis was that Jarod engaged in all these negative behaviors to escape the teasing and the anxiety of being in unfamiliar and what he felt to be unsafe places. We devised a very detailed plan, using context management strategies that reduced Jarod's contact with the general student body to almost nothing. We had him change classes, even in the pod, after the other kids did. We provided separate transportation and had him picked up at a quiet, previously unused exit of the building. He came to school a few minutes after the final bell and left just before school was dismissed. We even met with the other students and taught them about differences and what made Jarod so special. Many of the students knew Jarod's ability in math was superior to their own, and the teachers made arrangements for Jarod to tutor them.

These strategies were designed to give the teachers time to teach Jarod the social skills he needed to become more integrated into the student body after his tenth-grade year. As I mentioned before, the pod project supported a counselor, and a class period was set aside in Jarod's schedule so he could attend a small-group social skills class. Specific lessons were identified, and a curriculum was purchased.

Things went on—life was good. I was no longer in touch with Jarod or the team. They had the plan and were going to implement it, right? Wrong! Almost two years to the day, early in September, I get the same frantic call: "Jarod's out of control!" Same behaviors, only much more intense. What do you think went wrong?

I came to the school, observed what was going on, and asked the team how the behavior plan was going that we'd implemented two years prior. You know what they said to me? WHAT BEHAVIOR PLAN? The new team didn't know a thing about it, and now Jarod was thrust into the general population as an eleventh grader. Further investigation revealed another very ugly truth: The context management strategies the pod team implemented worked so well that the team never followed through with anything else—no social skills groups, no new skills taught. Everything was now the same as it was before, only Jarod was bigger, meaner, and much more aggressive. Unfortunately, there was no going back for Jarod. He started to refuse school entirely, never graduating. Last I knew he was staying home watching TV and eating too much.

In my opinion, this borders on malpractice, if there were such a thing in our field. Having had the tools at our fingertips, with all the resources lined up, just not following through was a tragedy for this young man and his family. Remember: To achieve lasting behavior change, teaching must take place.

11

I Want That

Reinforcing Youngsters Strategically

Teaching new behaviors takes time, sometimes a lot of time. So this next set of targeted interventions is designed to get rapid control over behaviors so that the youngster has problem-free opportunities in which to learn new skills.

Reinforcement strategies are very effective in changing behaviors; you just have to have something strong enough to motivate a youngster to behave as you would like him or her to do. That in itself can be a real challenge these days. Even more important, strategic reinforcement does not teach new behaviors. It only serves as a motivator. Keep in mind that NOTHING will ever substitute for teaching new skills.

Natural and Noncontingent Reinforcement

Many teachers complain about having to "pay students off" to behave and simply wish kids would do what's right. If you're saying this, what you're really saying is that you want kids to be NATURALLY reinforced as opposed to artificially reinforced. I'd like that, too. But I daresay you wouldn't come to work if you weren't receiving a paycheck at the end of every two weeks, now would you?

Humans don't do things "just because." We get something out of our work: pleasure, pride, money.. I'm not really crazy about spending all this time in front of my computer writing this book. And I don't write it because I'll earn so much money from the royalties (believe me). I write it because, once I'm finished with it, I am bound to learn more about what I like doing. I have organized my thoughts and experiences in a different, more concrete form. Ultimately, it makes me a better trainer, consultant, and mentor.

Whatever the motivator (i.e., reinforcer), we ALL increase certain behaviors in order to receive the things we want and love. Whether the reinforcement is naturally occurring or contrived and artificial, reinforcement depends on the person and the situation. It would be absolutely wonderful if we all behaved in certain ways just because we liked what we are doing. But get a grip, guys!

Positive Reinforcement

Most teachers understand the general concepts behind reinforcement. Positive reinforcement occurs when you offer an incentive immediately following a behavior that ultimately increases that behavior in the future: POSITIVE means you add or make something available, and REINFORCEMENT means that the behavior increases. Keep these two points in mind as we go further. For a through explanation of reinforcement, I suggest consulting Alberto and Troutman's 2012 book *Applied Behavior Analysis for Teachers.*

Some teachers become disgruntled and say, "You're really just bribing a kid to do what you want him to do." However, in the PBS model, reinforcement has nothing to do with bribing anybody: It's just the natural order of things from a behaviorist's viewpoint. And, by the way, the word *bribe* has the connotation of inducing a person to do something that is corrupt or shady or illegal. That's nothing like what we are doing here.

Negative Reinforcement Versus Punishment

Although teachers use both negative reinforcement and punishment strategies every day, they tend to mix up the important difference between the two. Remember, positive reinforcement means you are adding something to INCREASE the occurrence of the desired behavior in the future. When you use negative reinforcement, you actually take something away in order to INCREASE the desired behavior.

Punishment, frequently mislabeled negative reinforcement, is technically quite different. It means that you are seeking to DECREASE a behavior. If you yell at a student when he texts in class, you are hoping to DECREASE texting-in-class behavior by adding yelling at him. Another example of punishment would be if you would take away a token a student has earned because she had a tantrum in class. You are seeking to DECREASE tantrums by taking away the token, which the student desires.

What Is Good for the Goose Is NOT Necessarily Good for the Gander

As I said before, we are ALL reinforced in some way for behavior that we often demonstrate. If not, we wouldn't engage in the behavior. WHAT the reinforcement is differs greatly. But the fact remains: We continue to behave in certain ways because we get some kind of payoff.

That being established, there are two very important factors to keep in mind when reviewing and identifying reinforcing consequences and using reinforcement strategies to change or reduce behavior problems:

1. What you like and want and what I like and want can be two entirely different things.

2. If EVERYTHING sucks in your world, "learning to wait" will be almost impossible.

Before I talk about differential schedules of reinforcement, I want to repeat what I said before: Many times, the kids who are having the most trouble in the classroom, in the school building, at home, and in the community are those youngsters who have very little positive stuff going on in their lives. What I mean is that their lives are not rich with what we consider to be naturally occurring, or noncontingent, reinforcement. If they seem to struggle with adult relationships, it may be that they don't trust adults because adults have let them down so often.

These kids are asked to earn everything, and when they try to behave in a proper manner, the promised reinforcement is often not there or is so delayed that it doesn't strongly link the kind of cause and effect that we want them to understand. Kids need an environment rich with good stuff, and the good stuff needs to be positive adult attention and love and respect. If you have that, the need for artificial reinforcement will be limited. For the most part, kids who need the most positive reinforcement from us are the kids that don't get it anywhere else. The good news is that we know how to use their need to our advantage. It isn't easy, but it frequently is the key to turning these kids' behavior around.

When it comes to increasing the occurrence of newly learned skills, slather positive reinforcement on like you would ointment on a scraped knee. Do whatever it takes to be VERY CLEAR to a youngster that how he or she is behaving is EXACTLY what you want. There is no real strategy to this other than keeping the environment in which that youngster is living as rich with positive feedback as possible. When you've identified alternative behaviors to teach, reward them when the kid demonstrates them.

Decreasing Behavior with Reinforcement Strategies

When we're looking at behavior problems in the classroom setting, we generally want to reduce, not increase the behavior. Although there are many different types of reinforcement strategies, the two I include in almost every BIP are a Differential Reinforcement of Other Behavior (DRO) strategy or a modified version of a DRO called a Differential Reinforcement of Other Behaviors–Progressive (DROP) schedule, which I learned from Gary LaVigna and Tom Willis during an intensive training at the Institute for Applied Behavior Analysis in Los Angeles.

Let me write a disclaimer here and now: The reinforcement strategies that I am discussing here are simplified so that it is possible to use them in a classroom setting. Most strict behavioral methods were designed to be carried out in clinical settings, which give therapists a good deal more control over variables than a classroom teacher really has. I always keep the specific setting and students in mind when I write about these strategies. So if you're a purist, give me a break if my explanations are a less than perfect representation of the theoretical construct.

Also known as reinforcing the ABSENCE or nonoccurrence of the target behavior, differential reinforcement of either type—DRO or DROP—is used under the following conditions in a classroom setting:

1. The target behavior needs to be totally eliminated rather than reduced to a more acceptable level.

2. Reinforcement is available to the target student if the behavior is not displayed for a specified interval of time. (Intervals can be variable or fixed.)

3. The student receives the reinforcement if the target behavior does not occur REGARDLESS of any other problems that are present during that interval. For example, if the reinforcement is a piece of candy, the target behavior is "kicking," and the youngster spits during the interval but doesn't kick, technically he or she earns the candy. (Don't fret. You can always build in a slight, and I mean very slight delay, to avoid reinforcing spitting behavior.)

Don't confuse DROs and Reinforcement of Alternative Behavior (ALT-R) or Reinforcement of Incompatible Behavior (ALT-I) schedules because they are very different. DROs reinforce ONLY the absence of the problem. The other two approaches reinforce what the kid did instead. This is not to say you should not use these other strategies. Quite the opposite. But I believe ALT-R and ALT-I strategies should be used so frequently and intensely in the natural environment that you can't take data on their effectiveness. Not only CAN you take data when using a DRO, documenting when the reinforcement has been given becomes a data product. A DRO provides very clear boundaries to a student as to what he or she should NOT do. ALT-R and ALT-I give him or her a myriad of choices and sometimes require high levels of thinking and restraint, which may or may not be in the youngster's repertoire.

There are some cautions in using the DRO strategy. First, you may inadvertently reinforce another problem behavior that occurs before reinforcement. Second, you may teach the kid when he or she can demonstrate the behavior and still get access to the reinforcement. For example, let's say you have a kid on a 30-minute interval DRO for the target behavior of "swearing." You're asking her to refrain from swearing for a total amount of 30 minutes BEFORE she can have the reward. You set the timer for 30 minutes, she earns the reinforcement, you set the timer again for 30 minutes, and she swears like a sailor for 30 seconds. Oops, the problem occurred, you reset the timer for 30 minutes, and she behaves until the timer goes off again. She gets the reinforcement, you reset the timer, she swears like a sailor for 30 seconds, you reset the timer…and so it goes. In this case, you have actually TAUGHT the kid to swear after she gets the reward! Swearing doesn't cost the kid anything. She still earns as much of the reinforcement as was available for that school day.

The example I just described uses what is called a "reset," or variable, interval strategy: Every time the target behavior occurs, the timer is set again. What to do, what to do? Frankly, in the classroom, a reset format is hard to pull off and still conduct the rest of your teaching. Fixed intervals are standard time intervals that can be set with teaching convenience in mind. While there is such a thing as a Differential Reinforcement of Low Rates of Behavior (DRL) and other reinforcement models, these are better suited to the clinical setting.

I think a Differential Reinforcement of Other Behavior–Progressive, or DROP, schedule works very well in a school and classroom setting, however. This method allows much more freedom when creating just the right fit for the student and the staff. DROP schedules can be very effective because they make it very expensive to screw up. They also work for youngsters with significant cognitive disabilities or other severe difficulties.

Here's how the DROP approach works with our student, Martha.

Case Study: Martha

Martha, age 12, is in a self-contained classroom for students considered to be emotionally disturbed. Her target behavior is "disruption," defined as leaving her seat or assigned area without permission, bothering her peers by poking them, and making noises. These behaviors are most apparent during independent work periods that involve reading skills and math computation but sometimes occur during other activities. The functional hypothesis about this behavior is that it occurs to meet her need to escape tasks and expectations that she finds difficult or boring.

Martha LOVES working on crafts and art projects. She loves it so much that she doodles and draws in her books and notebooks most of the day. Given the opportunity, she would constantly use the materials the teacher has gathered in the back of the room (markers, sequins, fabric, cardboard, colored pencils, colored paper, glitter, glue) to create elaborate projects. These are not materials that she has readily available at home or in any other setting, so they are extremely valuable to her.

Mr. Gordon, Martha's teacher, has designed a system in which Martha can earn time in the craft area. Martha and Mr. Gordon identified the times in the daily schedule that are the most difficult for Martha to stay focused and to ask for help when she needs it. Each day there are three such periods. Martha knows that she will earn tokens, each representing one minute, for NOT being disruptive during these times. Also, there is a "free choice" period toward the end of every school day lasting about 15 minutes. It would be during this period that Martha could redeem the tokens representing minutes to access the craft materials.

Martha's program, briefly described, is as follows:

- Martha will earn tokens for not being disruptive during class. "Disruptive" behavior means she will not leave her seat or assigned area without permission and she will not bother her peers by poking and making noises.

- Martha is able to earn tokens duing all five independent work times during the day. These times will be noted on her individual daily schedule that she keeps on top of her desk.

- Each token equals one minute of free time.

- Martha will use her earned tokens to access all the craft materials located in the craft area in the back of the classroom.

- Martha must redeem her tokens at the end of each day.

Figure 16 describes Martha's DROP schedule. In the first period of the sequence, Martha can earn one token, or one minute, for NOT being disruptive, as defined above. In the next CONSECUTIVE period that Martha is NOT disruptive, she can earn two tokens, or two minutes. Having previously earned one minute from the first earning opportunity, she would then have a total of three tokens equaling a total of three minutes of craft time. In the third CONSECUTIVE interval she can earn three tokens. When combined with the other three tokens, this equals six minutes total for craft time. From that point on, each consecutive interval she is not disruptive, she can earn three tokens.

However, if Martha fails to earn tokens in an interval by being disruptive, the next interval that she is not disruptive she would earn only one token. This means she would need to earn her tokens in consecutive intervals once again to get the most tokens possible. This progressive situation makes it very expensive for Mar-

FIGURE 16 Martha's DROP Schedule

1. If Martha is disruptive during independent work time, she will earn zero tokens.

2. If Martha is NOT disruptive during independent work time, she will earn one token.

3. If Martha is NOT disruptive during the NEXT independent work time, she will earn two tokens.

4. From then on, if Martha is NOT disruptive during the NEXT independent work times, she will earn three tokens.

5. If Martha IS disruptive during independent work time, she will earn zero tokens.

6. Then she will start earning tokens again.

Independent work session	# of tokens earned
1	1
2	2
3	3
4	3
5	3
Total minutes possible for free time	12

tha to mess up and become disruptive. If she messes up, for example, during the third inteval, instead of six minutes of craft time, she would earn only three.

Figure 17 is Martha's data sheet, representing how many tokens/minutes she earned in a single day. You can see that by being disruptive during the third independent work session, Martha actually reduced her craft time by half. This shows how expensive the behavior can be. If the reinforcement is strong enough, it can provide a constant reminder to Martha to keep it together.

Finally, I have to say I often encounter resistance from teachers when attempting to build in DRO and DROP schedules into BIPs. This is especially true when there is only one teacher and 20 kids. It's hard to put these strategies into practice. But they do provide rapid control, and if carefully designed with both the teacher's and student's needs in mind, they can work nicely.

FIGURE 17 Martha's Data Sheet

Independent work session	# tokens available IF not disruptive
1	1
2	2
3	0
4	1
5	2
Total minutes free time earned	6

Sirens Are Blaring

Emergency Management Strategies

The final piece of the behavior plan is where most people start and finish. It's the answer to the question "What do I do if the student does _____?" That really translates to "What reactive strategies should I use?" These reactions are what "normal" kids understand and respond to: redirection and punishment.

Anticipatory Strategies

Before I list reactive strategies, however, I write a list of what I call "anticipatory strategies." These are the things you do PROACTIVELY when you start seeing Level 2 and 3 precursor behaviors in the youngster's Escalation and De-escalation Cycle. Take another look at Tommy, the Tasmanian Devil, first mentioned in chapter 4. His target behavior is "aggression," but it doesn't start until he has made physical contact. The first three levels of his cycle are as follows:

Level 1: Tommy is smiling, is very chatty with others, and can be easily redirected to an activity with minimal teacher interactions.

Level 2: Tommy is not smiling; he makes comments about another student or group of students who are not treating him fairly.

Level 3: Tommy's face is contorted in an angry sort of way. His eyes may be welling up with tears. He is pointing at other kids and accusing them of being cruel and unkind, calling him "stupid" or "dumb." He makes threatening comments such as "I'm going to get you" or "You guys can't beat me up."

When Tommy starts to make comments and complain that he isn't being treated well, what redirections would help him return to a Level 1 state? In other words, what could be put in place systematically to PREVENT the occurrence of the target behavior? Here's are some ideas:

1. Give him a previously agreed upon signal that he should stop and think.

2. Allow him a minute or two to put his head down.

3. Go over to him and remind him what he's earning in a gentle, nonthreatening way.

4. Let him have a predetermined number of "I need a break" cards that he can turn in and use as needed. (Each break card would provide a designated amount of time away.)

Anticipatory strategies need to be designed specifically for the student with whom you're working. They have to meet the immediate need without causing more trouble later. These strategies, like all external supports, need to be adjusted and faded carefully.

Remember little Jack in chapter 6? One note on Figure 11, the second A-B-C Checklist the teacher filled out, indicated that Jack had bitten someone severely after someone a provided a full physical prompt. Probing the situation a little more, I found out that Jack bit the teacher AFTER the full physical prompt was initiated. Like many youngsters with autism, Jack didn't like to be touched and found touching particularly offensive when he was upset and agitated. An anticipatory strategy for Jack included NOT touching him if he escalated to Level 3, if at all possible. If an adult finds touching necessary because Jack is becoming a threat to himself or others, that person should BE PREPARED! Jack will likely escalate immediately to a full-blown incident of physical aggression.

Reactive Strategies

Of course, most behavior plans aren't perfect. The target behavior is a learned response that has been a well-established part of a kid's behavioral repertoire for a long time. It's how the kid has gotten his or her needs met. There will be mistakes, and the youngster will need to receive REACTIVE consequences (i.e., punishment) because that's the culture of schools. And yes, folks, what you're doing is punishment regardless of how you assuage your conscience by calling it by any other name.

School policies and rules play a big part in what you list for reactive strategies, especially if the behavior is very severe. While children on IEPs may receive some accommodations when infractions directly related to their disability occur, some type of unpleasant consequence still needs to happen. But there must be a significant amount of caution.

Punishments may escalate a situation to a real crisis level. Or punishments may have an immediately favorable effect, but over the long run they could damage a relationship between the teacher and child to such a degree that the rift can't be repaired and the youngster no longer makes progress with that teacher.

It has been my experience that any reactive strategy you use for a kid with serious problems is good only for getting the problem resolved enough to reduce any danger or crisis that might occur. Reactive strategies teach very little, and they typically don't decrease the occurrence of the problem in the future. After all, you've tried these strategies many times before, but the problem still occurs and in many cases becomes more frequent. A very wise man once said that the definition of insanity is doing the same thing over and over again and expecting a different result.

All you can hope for with reactive strategies is some rapid and safe control. Once a crisis has passed, it's time to look at exactly what happened from start to finish and see where the plan failed. The good news is that if you write a plan that has multiple components, you don't have to rely on reactive or anticipatory strategies to change or reduce the target behavior. I used to tell my staff of teachers that if you find yourself reacting to a problem all the time, you have lost the battle. Even strategic reinforcements are, at best, just a way to accelerative positive behavior change. Eliminate them too soon, and the behavior will most likely return in full force.

In reality, the behavior war is played and won by teaching new skills. Skills instruction, along with careful context and environmental management, can change kids' lives for the better. Remember: We are teachers. It is what we do.

Epilogue

Have faith.

The fact that you're reading this book means you want to do the right thing. You're searching for a way that is REALLY possible. Knowing all the overwhelming responsibilities on your plate, I give you these ideas because I want things to be easier for you. I end the book with several BIP examples, included in Appendix B. These examples are a compilation of many of the cases my colleagues and I have worked on over the past 15 years. You may have noticed that most are younger students because that has been my focus over the years. However, these principles work for all ages (including spouses!). The names have been changed. Some are more recent than others. I hope you will use them to generate some ideas about the youngsters you know best.

As I said in chapter 1, I want you to work with this model and start to THINK differently. Always think about WHY. And keep your answer black and white: What's to be gained, and what's to be avoided? Once you know that, you can answer the question "What do I need to TEACH?" Practice this sequence of thinking daily. I guarantee you it will change the way you work with kids in such a positive way that you'll be sorry it took so long to figure out.

Finally, I have faith in you even if you have none in yourself. You're in this business to help kids. But start by helping yourself and remember K.I.S.S....Keep It Simple, Sweetheart.

Appendix A

Reproducible Forms

Behavior Concerns and Priorities Checklist

Student _____ Date _____

Problem behaviors			Priority
1. Absent frequently	Yes	No	
2. Aggressive	Yes	No	
3. Angry	Yes	No	
4. Bossy	Yes	No	
5. Bullies peers	Yes	No	
6. Defiant	Yes	No	
7. Disobedient	Yes	No	
8. Disruptive	Yes	No	
9. Disturbed	Yes	No	
10. Doesn't follow directions	Yes	No	
11. Emotionally high and low	Yes	No	
12. Forgetful	Yes	No	
13. Hyperactive	Yes	No	
14. Impulsive	Yes	No	
15. Laughs inappropriately	Yes	No	
16. Lazy	Yes	No	
17. Makes noises	Yes	No	
18. Off task	Yes	No	
19. Oppositional	Yes	No	
20. Out of area	Yes	No	
21. Out of seat	Yes	No	
22. Poor peer relations	Yes	No	
23. Screams/yells	Yes	No	
24. Spits	Yes	No	
25. Swears	Yes	No	
26. Talks out	Yes	No	
27. Tantrums/meltdowns	Yes	No	
28. Tardy frequently	Yes	No	
29.	Yes	No	
30.	Yes	No	

Scatter Plot Data Form

Student _____ Dates _____

Record each occurrence of the target behavior with a hash mark by day and class/activity/teachers. Total the number of occurrences each day and calculate an average for the day or week.

Class/activity/teachers	Monday	Tuesday	Wednesday	Thursday	Friday	Comments
Total responses						Average incidents per ☐ day or ☐ week _____

Interval Data Form

Student _____   Dates _____

Mark an X in the box if the behavior occurs ANY TIME during that period. Mark an O if it does not.

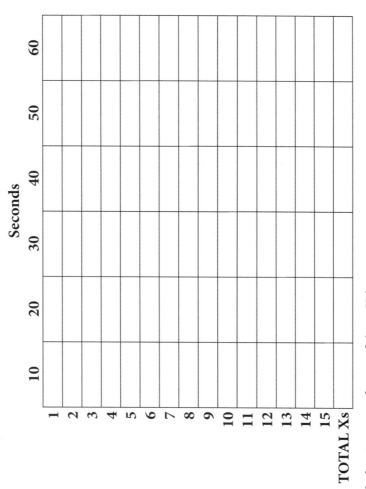

Seconds

	10	20	30	40	50	60
1						
2						
3						
4						
5						
6						
7						
8						
9						
10						
11						
12						
13						
14						
15						
TOTAL Xs						

Number of intervals behavior was observed (i.e., Xs): _____

Number of intervals in total observation period: _____

Rate of behavior (Xs / total no. of intervals observed) = _____

Time-Sampling Data Form

Student _____ Date _____

Mark an X in the box if the behavior occurs ANY TIME during that period. Mark an O if it does not.

Minutes

	10	20	30	40	50	60
1						
2						
3						
TOTAL Xs						

Number of intervals behavior was observed (i.e., Xs): _____

Number of intervals in total observation period: _____

Rate of behavior (Xs / total no. of intervals observed) = _____

Antecedents and Consequences Checklist

Student _____ Date _____

Use the back of this sheet to document any other triggers or consequences not listed.

Setting Events and Behavior Triggers		Immediate Consequences	
1. Academic demands/activities		1. Allowed access to preferred activity	
2. Academic failure		2. Assigment modified	
3. Allergies		3. Attention from adult	
4. Asked to wait		4. Attention from peers	
5. Conflicts at home		5. Given a break	
6. Conflicts at lunch time		6. Ignored by adults	
7. Conflicts during recess		7. Ignored by peers	
8. Conflicts in the hallway		8. Loss of privileges	
9. Conflicts on the bus		9. Moved to another area in classroom	
10. Correction received from adults		10. Peer support provided	
11. Difficult tasks		11. Personal time-out	
12. Easy tasks		12. Physical prompting	
13. Given multiple directions at one time		13. Provided physical reminders	
14. Hunger		14. Reaction from others	
15. Ignored		15. Reinforcement removed	
16. Illness		16. Seat changed	
17. Isolation from peers		17. Sent to hallway	
18. Long tasks		18. Sent to in-school support	
19. Missed/changed medication		19. Sent to office	
20. Negative peers		20. Sent to resource room	
21. Pain		21. Time-out given	
22. Physical effort		22. Takes a walk	
23. Preferred activities taken away			
24. Sensory overload			
25. Sleep problems			
26. Transitions		**Secondary Consequences**	
27. Working without a break		1. Expulsion	
28. Working with a peer		2. Out-of-school suspension	
29. Working independently		3. In-school suspension	
30. Working in a small group		4. Detention	
31. Working in a large group		5. Parent contacted	
32. Working away from desk		6. None	

From *Behavior Intervention Without Tears: Keeping FBAs and BIPs Simple*, © 2014 by Terri Chiara Johnston, Champaign, IL: Research Press (800-519-2707, www.researchpress.com)

A-B-C Recording Form

Name _____ Dates _____

Date	Antecedent								Behavior				Consequence											Comments
Totals																								

School Context Analysis Form

Student _____ Date _____

Class/activity/teachers	0–Never	1–Rarely	2–Sometimes	3–Often	4–Always

From *Behavior Intervention Without Tears: Keeping FBAs and BIPs Simple*, © 2014 by Terri Chiara Johnston, Champaign, IL: Research Press (800-519-2707, www.researchpress.com)

Functional Hypothesis Statement Form

Student_____Date_____

Target behavior: _____

Description: _____

_____

Start Time: _____

_____

Stop Time: _____

_____

1. What is the one event, demand, situation, person, etc. that will trigger the behavior IMMEDIATELY?

   _____

   _____

2. Fill in the blanks.

   _____ (student's name) engages in

   _____ (name the

   behavior) in order to GAIN ACCESS TO / ESCAPE OR AVOID (circle only one)

   _____

   _____

   _____ (name what and where).

From *Behavior Intervention Without Tears: Keeping FBAs and BIPs Simple,* © 2014 by Terri Chiara Johnston, Champaign, IL: Research Press (800-519-2707, www.researchpress.com)

Appendix B

FBA and BIP Examples

When it comes to writing good Functional Behavior Assessments and effective Behavior Intervention Plans, less is best...always.

Whatever format you use, how you present the information, whether you attach the FBA/BIP to an IEP or another document is all up to your state and federal guidelines. However, there are some important factors that must be addressed for your documents to be effective.

An FBA must provide a clear description of the target behavior in measurable terms. To count a behavior, a clearly defined beginning and ending must be established—in other words, Start and Stop Time. Finally, a hypothesis stating whether the youngster is escaping or avoiding an event or trying to gain access to an event or tangible item is necessary. It's also helpful to note what is being escaped or what the child is trying to gain access to.

A BIP must have five components in order to be effective:

1. Identification of new skills and behaviors that need to be taught to replace a challenging behavior

2. Directions identifying which contexts or environments need to be altered to avoid problems altogether

3. Strategic reinforcement programs that motivate a student to use newly taught behaviors

4. Ways to anticipate and predict problems BEFORE they start

5. What to do when a challenging behavior occurs

If you create a BIP that includes these components, you will be surprised how many problem will disappear with a few weeks. The youngster will experience success, and we know that success begets success, don't we? Practice makes perfect. Try the system out and consult with one another. This keeps your mind fresh and creative.

Included in this appendix are assessments and resulting behavior intervention plans that my colleague Sandra Haltrich and I wrote over the years. I have kept the format relatively simple because it is not the format but the content that is important. Change the titles, change the organization—change anything you want—as long as the information is included.

Tony's FBA/BIP

Target Behavior

Description

"Defiance, disrespect," defined as refusing to complete an activity or follow an academic direction (e.g., "You can't make me do it," "No," "I hate you," whining, etc.). On rare occasions, behavior will escalate to uncontrollable crying, negative statements such as "I hate this. I don't want to be alive." These behaviors typically occur during or right before academic instruction or when Tony is expected to complete independent assignments.

Start and Stop Time

The behavior starts when Tony refuses to follow a specific teacher direction within 60 seconds and/or begins making negative and inappropriate comments to the teacher. The behavior stops when he is engaged in a specified activity for at least five minutes.

Escalation and De-escalation Cycle

Escalation behavior may include Tony's ignoring a teacher; playing with objects in the area; clenching fists; grabbing his hair; clenching teeth; crying; yelling, "I'm frustrated. I can't do this"; etc. De-escalation behaviors include calming down, stopping crying, and asking for help.

FUNCTIONAL HYPOTHESIS STATEMENT

The function of Tony's defiance and disrespectful comments is to escape/avoid academic demands.

IMPRESSIONS

Strengths

- Tony can be very polite.

- He has a highly developed sense of humor.

- His teacher reports that he has several friends in the fourth-grade class and does well at recess.

- Tony appears to respect and respond to the classroom point system.

- He uses a daily schedule to keep himself organized.

Areas Requiring Intervention

- Academic skills are assessed to be significantly below grade level in all areas of instruction.

- Tony demonstrates a very low tolerance for frustration, frequently giving up rather than persevering.

- He does not maintain attention when engaged in academic tasks.

- Tony appears to be very lethargic and frequently refuses to engage in any movement activities.

- He appears to be very immature for his age, yet is reported to have friends at school.

- His ability to process sensory input appears to be problematic and may be affecting his ability to modulate his responses.

Special Notes/Considerations

Tony has a long history of behavior and academic problems. He lives with his grandmother, Mrs. _____, but visits his mother regularly. Unfortunately, his relationship with his mother and two younger siblings appears to be chaotic and unstable. Mrs. Johns has reported that he may feel abandoned by his mother who, due to Tony's significant emotional problems, is unwilling or incapable of raising him on her own.

Tony has never been in a regular classroom setting. He appears to do best under the highest level of structure and academic support. In addition, Tony has been seen by numerous psychiatrists and psychologists, as well as placed in different separate educational facilities. Although medication has been prescribed, it appears that the trials have not been long enough to assess effectiveness. He has been assessed on numerous occasions and is currently receiving an independent evaluation from a private provider.

Mental health diagnoses have included bipolar disorder, attention deficit disorder, and oppositional defiant disorder. Dr. _____ added to the diagnosis on June 4, 20__ by diagnosing him with pervasive developmental disorder. Regardless, his behavioral issues are the same now as they were in the beginning of his school career.

Behavior Intervention Plan

Skills Instruction

- Tony should receive social skills instruction and practice daily in context.

- Direct instruction in the area of cause and effect should be provided; use of social situations as well as academic application is important.

- Direct instruction in attribution formation and analysis should occur, focusing on creating an internal motivation that is rewarded through effort.

Environmental Changes

- Creating defined behavioral boundaries and expectations is critical to Tony's success.

- Within the school context, Tony should experience consistent, concrete feedback as to the appropriateness of his behavior throughout the day.

- Tony's schedule should be Premacked in such a way that he gains access to his desired activities and reinforcement only when he has met academic expectations.

- Academic instruction should be carefully calibrated to his instructional level: not too hard, not too easy—just right (also known as the "Goldilocks Rule").

- Verbal instructions and communication with Tony should be significantly reduced in terms of quantity; staff should be particularly aware of his perception of humor and teasing because he is very likely to overstep his boundaries and be unaware of how inappropriate he is with authority figures.

- Increasing the print size and decreasing the amount of information on a given worksheet may help to reduce Tony's academic frustration and increase his willingness to try new things.

- Paper-and-pencil tasks should be decreased, while functional application of concepts could increase his ability to perform tasks.

- As much as possible, efforts to increase Tony's purposeful movement should be made; movement should NOT be a choice for him but part of academic or behavioral expectations.

Differential Reinforcement of Other Behavior (DRO)

At the beginning of each day, Tony will choose a reinforcer from a preestablished reinforcer menu and place a picture of his selection on the "I am working for _____" board. If Tony has received _____ [number of] tokens at the end of the day, he may access the selected reinforcer. After _____ days, Tony will need to earn more tokens in order to acquire the desired reinforcer.

Data collection should consist of the number of intervals he earns a token out of the number of intervals the token is available.

Anticipatory Responses

As soon as any of the precursor behaviors occurs, Tony should be directed away from the task for at least 60 seconds. He should be directed to take deep breaths and count to 20. Once that has been accomplished and he appears calm, he may be asked if he's ready to continue. He should be reminded that he MUST complete all activities for the designated period on his schedule before he can proceed to the next scheduled activity.

Reactive Strategies

If Tony engages in the target behavior, staff should react in as nonemotional a way as possible. They should not engage him verbally or remind him that he is not earning his reinforcement until he is in full compliance again. If he places himself or the staff in an unsafe situation, other staff members should be called in for support, but there should be NO conversation with Tony or among the staff. Once Tony is under control for at least five minutes, staff can engage him in verbal mediation and indicate that he did not earn his tokens and that he is expected to complete the assignment.

> *This plan should remain in effect for at least two weeks prior to changing any item or procedure and must only be changed with the agreement of the education team.*

Shirley's FBA/BIP

TARGET BEHAVIOR

Description

"Aggression, " defined as hitting, slapping, swatting, pulling hair, throwing objects, pushing, or shoving.

Start and Stop Time

The behavior is considered started when any of the above occurs, and the behavior is considered ended when none of the above behaviors are exhibited and when Shirley has been engaged in a teacher-directed activity or direction for five minutes or more.

Escalation and De-escalation Cycle

Shirley begins to rock, closes her eyes, and hums. When she hums louder and louder, and may start to get up and look at a student or her attendant. After the incident, she sits in an assigned area, rocking and looking at people. She may cry. As she calms down, her tears stop and she stops humming. Eventually, she stops rocking. At that point she can receive direction.

FUNCTIONAL HYPOTHESIS STATEMENT

The function of Shirley's aggression, as defined, is escape or avoidance of teacher demands, particularly academic tasks.

IMPRESSIONS

Strengths

- Shirley prefers to engage in functional daily living tasks that are meaningful to her rather than academic lessons.

- Shirley loves to listen to music.

- Shirley is interested in Disney characters, particularly Mickey Mouse.

- Shirley enjoys deep sensory input.

- Shirley loves to walk and move her body.

- Shirley appears to have a good receptive vocabulary.

Areas Requiring Intervention

- Shirley's expressive communication is seriously compromised.

- Shirley's aggressive behavior is negatively affecting her educational experience.

- Shirley has difficulty tolerating peers or adults in close proximity.

- Shirley has difficulty remaining seated in many activities.

- Shirley prefers to be in an isolated area.

- Shirley has difficulty when asked to restrict her movements.

- Shirley is not interested in typical academic activities.

Special Notes/Considerations

Shirley has had access to an alternative communication device for some time. The problem has been getting her to use it functionally. She has been known to do so but frequently uses the device to express her interest in Mickey Mouse and other Disney characters instead.

BEHAVIOR INTERVENTION PLAN

Skills Instruction

- Shirley needs to learn an alternative communication method to use when she is anxious or upset so that others are able to understand what she wants, thus reducing her need to become aggressive.

- Shirley needs to learn to access deep pressure (e.g., forehead and chin presses, etc.) without becoming aggressive.

- Shirley's course of study should focus on social skills instruction, prevocational behavioral instructions, and functionally embedded instruction.

- Shirley must learn appropriate social skills to gain access to time away from the group, request a break from a task or movement, and communicate refusal.

- Shirley needs to learn independent self-management and daily living skills.

- Shirley needs to learn prevocational skills (e.g., attending to tasks, working independently, completing tasks on time, following directions from a supervisor, etc.).

Environmental Changes

- Shirley should have an augmentative and alternative communication (AAC) "check-up" evaluation focused on whether the current device is still the optimal choice for communication support at this time.

- Shirley's day should be tightly structured in a clear "first-then" contingency format. Her access to escape from adults should be contingent upon her demonstration of appropriate social behavior. Preferred activities should be available to Shirley when her immediate behavior warrants.

- Shirley should practice the expected behavior through opportunities set up by teachers throughout the day.

- A stimulus-control program should be implemented to give Shirley a clear, visual signal indicating when attention is available and when it is not.

- Concrete and consistent feedback regarding her behavior is critical in getting Shirley ready for transition to high school and postgraduation environments.

- Shirley's schedule should include only functionally embedded activities that are rich in naturally occurring reinforcement.

- Purposeful movement activities will be necessary for Shirley to be successful in all environments.

Differential Reinforcement of Other Behavior (DRO)

The absence of the target behavior, as defined, will be reinforced. The day should be broken down into 15-minute intervals. At the beginning of the period, Shirley will choose a reinforcer from a preestablished menu and place a picture of her selection on the "I am working for _____" board.

- Start the timer. When the timer goes off and behavior has not occurred, show Shirley the icon and say, "You kept your hands to yourself. You get _____."

- If the behavior has occurred, show Shirley the icon and say, "You did not keep your hands to yourself. Try again" and reset the timer.

Data should consist of the number of intervals per day Shirley earns her reinforcer.

Emergency Management

- If Shirley is having a difficult day, reduce all environmental stimuli and demands as much as possible.

- With a gesture, remind Shirley what she is earning.

- If Shirley engages in the target behavior, she must be contained with the least amount of attention possible. No verbal interaction whatsoever should take place.

- Parents should be informed after school via a home communication notebook or email after Shirley has engaged in the target behavior. It would be extremely helpful if Shirley's access to preferred activities be denied that evening.

This plan should be attached to the IEP and remain in effect for at least four weeks prior to changing any item or procedure.

Irving's FBA/BIP

TARGET BEHAVIOR

Description

"Physical aggression," defined as the presence of one or more of the following: knocking furniture over; banging chair on floor; throwing and/or clearing school supplies from tables; hitting, pushing, poking, pinching, head butting, scratching, biting, or otherwise inflicting pain or harm to another individual.

Start and Stop Time

Behavior starts when Irving makes contact with another individual or throws items, knocks over furniture, and/or clears items from tabletops. Behavior is considered stopped when Irving refrains from being physically aggressive for 10 minutes or longer.

Escalation and De-escalation Cycle

Escalation includes grimace on face, protest, vocalizing scream, jumping out of seat, jumping up and down, darting from area, darting toward staff, pulling on staff, covering ears with hands, rocking intensely back and forth in seat, falling out of chair or dropping to floor, flinging body around, putting fingers down throat, and attempting escape from designated area. De-escalation includes sitting in chair, having a calm body, looking toward staff, and complying with directions.

FUNCTIONAL HYPOTHESIS STATEMENT

Irving is attempting to escape high-demand situations and unstructured environments by becoming physically aggressive.

IMPRESSIONS

Strengths

- Can be responsive to repeated prompts that can be the basis of shaping functional behavior.

- Can be redirected with stimuli he finds motivating.

- Has the intellectual ability to develop educational skills.

- Is able to follow simple directions.

- Can respond to visual cues and verbal commands.

Areas Requiring Intervention

- Impulsive behavior.

- Inadequate social skills.

- Difficulties with attention and focus.

- Distractibility.

- Physical aggression/property destruction.

- Lack of modulation of mood and temperament.

- Excessive need for sensory stimulation.

- Gains from interventions but will progress slowly and, at times, inconsistently.

- Generalization will not occur rapidly and therefore reinforcement schedules will have to be applied on an individual and restricted basis.

BEHAVIOR INTERVENTION PLAN

Skills Instruction

- Direct instruction in following a daily schedule should be provided.

- A cueing system should be used to give Irving an awareness of time remaining prior to transitioning.

- Initially, a "first-then" schedule will provide Irving clear expectations and predictions of what comes next.

- Direct instruction using a pictorial representation of "Wait" will be proactively incorporated into Irving's daily schedule.

- Direct instruction will be provided to help Irving follow sequential, step-by-step task analysis of specific functional academics (e.g., classroom routines, vocational tasks, activities providing planned motor movement throughout the building, and self-help skills).

- Direct instruction will be provided in following a sensory routine that provides choices of predictable activities, represented pictorially and with printed words. It is recommended that two routines be constructed to give Irving the opportunity to make a choice.

- Any sensory activities/routines should be approved by the district's licensed occupational therapist.

- Direct instruction should move from working one on one with staff to working independently in a structured work system area.

- Direct instruction should follow behavioral cue cards for expected behaviors within all school settings.

- Verbal and visual feedback should be provided to distinguish between Irving's target behavior and what is deemed appropriate in that social circumstance. For example, if Irving seeks a teacher's attention by grabbing or pinching her, staff should firmly reestablish the physical boundary and state the appropriate way for him to request attention. Attention should then be withheld until he follows the provided model.

Environmental Changes

- A master schedule should be posted in Irving's area to provide consistency among all staff members.

  Irving's "first-then" schedule should be represented pictorially as a two-inch icon and a printed word.

  Visual cueing and a timer should be provided to enable Irving to transition from one activity to the next.

  The "Wait" icon should be similarly represented.

  Construct task analysis for all items.

  Construct sensory routines, represented pictorially and with printed word.

- Irving requires access to an area where he can receive intense sensory stimulation, such as deep compressions and other sensory protocols as identified by the district's licensed occupational therapist. These should be presented noncontingently and aimed at reducing his need for excessive motor activity and aggression.

- Nonstructured classroom activities should be replaced with more structured project boxes such as those found in a TEACCH environment.

- Open spaces should be avoided; instead, an environment of close proximity to environmental elements should be maintained.

- A variety of gross motor activities, represented pictorially and with printed word, should be made available when Irving has time in the gymnasium.

Differential Reinforcement of Other Behavior (DRO)

For every 15-minute interval that Irving does NOT display the target behavior (i.e., physical aggression) as defined, he should receive a token or a puzzle piece of his desired tangible reinforcement (primary reinforcement, food/sensory).

- If tokens are used, when he receives two tokens he will cash them in for items he values and that have been identified as what he has been working for through his visual work system prior to every 15-minute interval.

- If the puzzle format is used, when the puzzle is complete (two pieces), he will receive the item designated by the puzzle (e.g., popcorn puzzle if he chooses popcorn or "squeezes" or "stretching," if that is his choice).

- When Irving receives his reinforcement, state, "Good job, safe hands." If Irving does not earn the reinforcement, the puzzle system starts over.

Data collection will consist of notations of number of intervals Irving earns his tokens or puzzle piece.

Anticipatory Responses

- Provide a mat or soft pad to protect Irving.

- Limit Irving's instruction area so he has less opportunity to escape.

- Provide boundaries for "choice" area and "sensory" area.

- Use a firm count (e.g., "I'm going to count to three, and you're going to _____. One, two, three").

- Do not try to lift Irving from a sitting or lying position.

- Continually remind Irving of what he's working for.

Reactive Strategies

- If Irving engages in the target behavior (i.e., physical aggression) or if he engages in property destruction and/or self-injurious behavior, staff will put him in the protective hold techniques designated by the district. Do not talk to Irving during the restraint until he is calm and quiet for at least three minutes. As soon as he is calm, give him a compliance drill (e.g., "Touch nose, touch ears, touch chin"). If he complies, direct him to the next activity, then reset Irving's token board.

- To analyze antecedents leading to the crisis, all incidents of aggression/property destruction and physical intervention must be recorded on the school crisis form and debriefed by staff no later than that day after school.

This plan should remain in effect for at least two weeks prior to changing any item or procedure and must only be changed with the agreement of the education team.

Johsua's FBA/BIP

TARGET BEHAVIOR

Description

"Tantrum," defined as the presence of one or more of the following: loud banging on desk with open hand or closed fist; running around the room, escaping area and running in hallway; jumping up and down; shouting or making utterances, animal sounds, and/or vocalizations; uncontrollable laughter; screaming; darting or aggressive charging at staff; kicking staff lower body with enough force to cause pain and bruising; scratching staff, hitting staff with open hand or closed fist with enough force to cause pain and/or bruising; banging on walls or doors; clearing items from desks/tables; using school equipment to hit; pushing desk into peers; pulling charts from walls; and kicking school equipment/supplies.

Start and Stop Time

Behavior starts when Joshua engages in one or more of the above in the description of tantrum. Behavior is considered stopped or over when Joshua refrains from the above tantrum, is sitting in a chair, engaged in an activity, for five minutes or longer.

Escalation and De-escalation Cycle

During escalation, Joshua pouts, has grimace on face, scans the classroom, searches through desk, drops school supplies to floor, inappropriately uses or fidgets with school equipment/supplies; refuses to participate in activity with peers, talk, or move to designated area; resists staff interventions; slaps head or thrusts head back and forth, possibly moving head in circular motion; begins tapping on hands or desk; refuses to engage in academic activity or follow classroom rules and/or routines. During de-escalation, Joshua becomes quieter and may still be looking around, but he doesn't make negative comments. His body becomes more relaxed, and he starts taking deep breaths on his own. Then he'll raise his hand to say he's ready.

FUNCTIONAL HYPOTHESIS STATEMENT

The function of the target behavior is twofold: (a) primary—escape/avoidance of nonpreferred academic demands and/or activities and (b) secondary—escape or avoidance of sensory assaults (e.g., unstructured activities/events requiring social interaction with peers).

IMPRESSIONS

Strengths

- Has the intellectual ability to develop educational skills.

- Is able to follow two- and three-step directions.

- Has the ability to reduce his level of frustration when redirected by the use of interesting and motivating materials.

- Can engage in interactions with friends and display sense of humor.

- Eager to please preferred adults.

- Articulate and polite when interacting with preferred adults.

Areas Requiring Intervention

- Difficulties with transitions and changes in daily routine.

- Poor organizational skills.

- Difficulties with attention and focus.

- Distractibility.

- Inadequate social skills.

- Lack of ability to recognize sensory triggers.

- Lack of modulation of mood and temperament.

- Tantrum behaviors.

- Lack of ability to handle anger, frustration, and/or disappointment.

- Generalization will not occur rapidly and therefore reinforcement schedules will have to be applied on an individual and restricted basis.

BEHAVIOR INTERVENTION PLAN

Skills Instruction

- Direct instruction focusing on Joshua's daily schedule and organizational skills is needed, to include instruction pertaining to self-management skills.

- A cueing system prior to transitioning should be established.

- A meaningful reinforcement menu board should be constructed for use with Joshua's behavior contract.

- Social skills instruction should include verbal and written scripts with adults and peers and involve role-playing the following situations:

  Expressing frustration, anger, and disappointment in an appropriate manner.

  Responding positively in crisis situation.

  Positive peer/adult interactions.

Initiating appropriate responses in a variety of situations.

Conflict resolution.

- Direct instruction should also be provided in the following areas:

Recognizing/verbalizing sensory triggers in a variety of environments.

Following a sensory routine approved by the district's licensed occupational therapist.

Following a prescribed problem-solving model: (a) identify the problem, (b) generate possible solutions, (c) predict consequences of each solution, (d) choose and implement a solution, (e) evaluate outcome.

Self-evaluating his performance in each classroom according to his "daily passport."

Following a behavior contract.

Making appropriate choices for activities to engage in during physical education class.

Recognizing feelings and initiation of self-calming activities.

Identifying other people's perceptions of him and his behaviors.

Environmental Changes

- A daily schedule should be completed, whether in printed form or on the computer. The times should correspond to each class, including free time, study hall, specials, and/or lunch. This schedule should be reviewed periodically throughout Joshua's day and items checked off to help improve Joshua's organizational skills.

- Joshua should be provided with a cueing system, visually represented, prior to any transitions. This cue could be cards representing the number "3" (meaning it is three minutes till time to stop an activity), the number "2," and the number "1" (indicating that it is time to transition).

- A menu board of sensory activities/equipment should be available for Joshua's sensory breaks. As possible, an area to engage in these activities should be provided (table in hallway, back of classroom, etc.).

- Prior to transitioning, Joshua should receive visual reminders to enable him to recognize sensory triggers in different environments, as follows: "I need help," "I need a break," and "I want to work alone." Prior to transitioning, staff should discuss these supports with Joshua. The "I need a break" card should specify what a break consists of (e.g., walk in hallway, get a drink, etc.).

- An area away from the group should be provided in the hallway or at a table with a study carrel for use when Joshua is engaged in academic tasks. Staff should offer Joshua the choice of working at his space or choosing a quiet area to work.

- Joshua should have social scripts for skill instruction. These scripts must be unique to Joshua's specific situation, describe what he is to do, how he is to do it, and what others will think and feel when he is able to follow his plan. Joshua should also have time to discuss positive statements and interactions with his peers.

- Joshua's "daily passport," which specifies the time of day and expected behavior within all school settings, combined with the recovery behavior, is currently in place. Joshua is given the opportunity to evaluate his performance throughout the day.

- A behavior contract should be constructed that addresses Joshua's target behavior ("tantrum"). In addition, other behaviors should be incorporated into his contract (e.g., remaining on task and practicing self-control in difficult situations). These are only suggestions and should be determined by the teaching team. The contract should clearly define the expectations for each behavior in detail. In addition, a self-evaluation component should be part of the contract.

This could be a scale from zero to three rating Joshua's performance. Ideally, staff should have a similar scale, rate Joshua, and compare that rating to his rating. This will help Joshua understand how others perceive his behaviors.

- Joshua should be provided with a menu board of reinforcers to support his behavior contract. It is important that reinforcers be meaningful to Joshua (e.g., computer time or access to a special game on the computer). Puzzles have been constructed to give Joshua a variety of choices of activities/items to work for. In addition, Joshua has expressed an interest in specific toys advertised in magazines provided by parents. As possible, he could earn tickets to purchase the items in these magazines. This plan should be discussed and approved by parents.

- Joshua should be provided with a menu board, pictorially representing alternative activities available during physical education.

- Joshua should be provided with a pictorial representation of a thermometer to help him recognize and identify feelings. This thermometer should be laminated and kept in Joshua's binder. He could help staff develop this meter to correctly identify how he feels, including both positive and negative feelings. Joshua could develop words to describe his feelings and exactly what makes him feel better, what relaxes him, and what sort of things fulfill his needs. He could then use this meter to discuss his feelings and the activities he needs to engage in for self-calming.

- A "chill area" within the classroom, in the hallway, or in the resource room would help Joshua engage in calming activities when he feels frustrated or anxious. A variety of materials could be provided to encourage drawing, identifying, and/or writing about how he is feeling.

- Throughout Joshua's day, it is important to point out what he is doing and how his friends feel about it. It is also important to recognize when he is acting inappropriately. Similarly, if Joshua is displaying appropriate social interactions in unstructured areas, he should be praised by staff and given reinforcement for such interactions.

Differential Reinforcement of Other Behavior (DRO)

For every 15-minute interval that Joshua does NOT display the targeted behavior ("tantrum"), he should receive a token. At the end of four successive intervals that he earns tokens, he may cash in his tokens for items he values and that his behavior contract specifies he has identified as "working for." In addition, he should complete an evaluation of his performance for each session. Items of interest to Joshua are the computer, fruit juice, a special computer game, and working with the custodian. All suggested reinforcers should be agreed upon with Joshua prior to implementing the program. When Joshua receives his reinforcement, staff should state, "Great job. you remained calm in the classroom and did not tantrum."

Data collection should consist of notations of number of intervals Joshua earns his tokens.

Anticipatory Responses

- Social reinforcement and very specific verbal praise should be given to Joshua whenever he is able to effectively engage in the strategies described in this BIP.

- Staff should remind Joshua of what he is working for throughout the day.

- Staff should remind Joshua of expected behaviors whenever he transitions.

Reactive Strategies

- If Joshua engages in the target behavior, staff should remove him to a quiet area (e.g., outside the classroom, on the bench, in the resource room) and, as possible, calm and mediate the situation. If Joshua engages in self-injurious behavior, property destruction, or physical aggression, strategies and guidelines outlined in the school's parent/student discipline code book should be employed.

- Staff should not talk to Joshua during a restraint until he is calm and quiet for at least five minutes.

- As soon as he is calm, staff should give Joshua a compliance drill. If he complies, staff should direct him to the next activity on his schedule and reset his token board.

- To analyze antecedents leading to the crisis, all incidents of aggression, self-injurious behavior, or property destruction must be recorded on the school crisis form and debriefed by staff no later than after school that day.

This plan should remain in effect for at least two weeks prior to changing any item or procedure.

Sally's FBA/BIP

TARGET BEHAVIOR

Description

"Tantrum," defined as becoming argumentative: volume of voice escalates, may shut down and refuse to do work and/or follow through with teacher interventions, voice volume will continue to increase to screaming, verbal protests will continue, crying (demonstrative tears).

Start and Stop Time

The behavior starts when Sally refuses to work within two minutes of a teacher direction. The behavior stops when she is engaged in a specified activity for at least 10 minutes.

Escalation and De-escalation Cycle

In escalation, Sally will be off task, visually scan the classroom, fidget in her seat, search through her desk, interject comments/demands, stop working and attempt to engage in alternative activity (usually reading), and ignore teacher directions. Sally will raise her hand for a question and ultimately debate teacher regarding independent work completion. De-escalation takes place when Sally stops all vocalizations and debates. She may sit idle for some time or start and stop the assignment. Finally, she begins to work without comments.

Functional Hypothesis Statement

The function of Sally's behavior is to gain access to power and control over her environment.

Impressions

Strengths

- Sally has a unique sense of humor.

- Sally enjoys reading.

- Sally functions in the superior range with regard to cognitive and academic skills.

- Sally responds well to adults in conversation.

Areas Requiring Intervention

- Sally resists undesirable activities and is easily overwhelmed by assignments, particularly written output, or tasks requiring sustained effort.

- Sally struggles with organizational skills.

- Physical education activities present a challenge to Sally.

- Sally is distractible and off task often during academic instruction and independent seat work.

- Sally has trouble stopping an activity and/or transitioning to a new activity.

- Sally's social skills are significantly impaired, as follows:

  Sally has not developed any close peer relationships with classmates.

Sally struggles with managing her temper and modulating her mood.

Sally struggles in structured small-group academics.

Sally has difficulty taking turns in group settings, remaining on topic, and acknowledging others' points of view.

Special Notes/Considerations

Sally has a longstanding history of challenging behaviors, particularly tantrums and noncompliance with teacher directives. Frequently, she will refuse teacher intervention and shut down. Sally exhibits work avoidance in most academic areas.

BEHAVIOR INTERVENTION PLAN

Skills Instruction

- Direct instruction focusing on Sally's daily schedule and organizational skills is needed throughout her day, to include instruction pertaining to self-management skills.

- Direct instruction is required in using a cueing system prior to transitioning and stopping activity.

- Direct instruction is required in following a protocol for physical education.

- Direct instruction in using visual cues is needed to help Sally stay focused on her work.

- Direct social skills instruction is needed in a group of two or more peers and/ or independently, focusing on the following areas:

Recognizing feelings and initiation of self-calming activities.

Expressing frustration, anger, and disappointment in an appropriate manner.

Engaging in positive social interactions with peers and taking turns and working cooperatively in small structured group settings.

Initiating appropriate responses in a variety of situations.

Conflict resolution.

- Instruction in the following problem-solving model should be provided: (a) identify the problem, (b) generate possible solutions, (c) predict consequences of each solution, (d) choose and implement a solution, (e) evaluate outcome.

- Direct instruction in how to follow a behavior checklist should be provided.

- Instruction should be given in identifying other people's perceptions of Sally and her behaviors.

Environmental Changes

- A daily schedule should be completed, whether in a print form or on the computer. This schedule should be reviewed periodically throughout Sally's day. Times should correspond to each class (including free time, lunch, etc.). This will help improve Sally's organizational skills. It is recommended that Sally cross out or check off each period as it is completed. Also, she should review this schedule in the morning and fill in any changes to occur for that day. Sally's schedule should be Premacked in such a way that she gains access to her desired activities and reinforcement only when she has met the social expectation.

- Sally should be provided with a cueing system, visually represented, prior to any transitions. This system could be an icon representing the number "3" (meaning three minutes), "2", and "1" (meaning finished).

- A visual protocol should be developed with the physical education teacher to assist Sally by giving her the ability to make choices.

- Visual cues should be provided to help Sally remain focused on her independent seat work.

- Behavioral feedback should be given with as little affect as possible. Sally should experience consistent, concrete feedback as to the appropriateness of her behavior throughout her school day.

- Social skills instruction should involve using verbal, written scripts with adults and peers, and engaging in role-play situations.

- An area should be designated for Sally to engage in self-calming/self-relaxation activities, as needed.

- A behavior checklist should be constructed, including Sally's target behavior. Sally's behavior checklist will focus on the following goals:

  Following directions given by the teacher and starting work within two minutes.

  Working cooperatively in groups, as follows: (a) without arguing/debating peers, (b) taking turns, and (c) remaining on topic.

- A menu board of reinforcers should be constructed with Sally to ensure that the reinforcement is meaningful to her.

Differential Reinforcement of Other Behavior (DRO)

At the beginning of each session, Sally will choose a reinforcer from a preestablished reinforcer menu board and write what her selection is on her behavioral chart. Sally will receive a check/ticket for each period designated on her schedule. Sally will receive the chosen reinforcer twice a day, prior to lunch and at the end of the school day. After _____ days, Sally will have to earn more checks/tickets in order to acquire the desired reinforcer.

Data consist of the number of intervals she earns a check/ticket out of the number of intervals the check/ticket is available.

Anticipatory Responses

- As soon as any of the precursor behaviors occurs, Sally should be asked to move to a quiet area and take a break. At this time, she could draw or complete a "feelings sheet." Once she has completed a sheet and is calm, she should be asked whether she is ready to continue.

- Staff should remind her that she must complete all work/activities for the designated period on her schedule before she can proceed to the next scheduled activity.

Reactive Strategies

- If Sally engages in the target behavior, she will be asked to return to the resource room or, if needed, escorted to the resource room. She will then be directed to the calming area to calm and complete a mediation sheet. Once Sally is under control for at least five minutes, staff can engage her in verbal mediation and indicate that she did not earn her check/ticket and that she is expected to complete her assignment.

This plan should remain in effect for at least four weeks prior to changing any item or procedure.

Alice's FBA/BIP

Target Behavior

Description

"Noncompliant/defiant behavior," defined as including a cluster of negative confrontational behaviors that occur over a period of time (two or more occurring together), as follows: refusal to follow teacher directions, verbal confrontation with adults, escaping area, running in the hallway, locking self in room or stall area of bathroom, refusing staff interventions, physical aggression directed toward staff, hitting with open hand/closed fist, refusing to follow classroom/school rules and routines.

Start and Stop Time

Behavior starts when any of the behaviors described occurs. Behavior is considered over when Alice becomes calm and quiet, is sitting in a chair, complies with an adult direction for 10 minutes or more, and is actively engaged in an activity.

Escalation and De-escalation Cycle

Escalation involves the following: Alice will engage in self-talk, pout, scan the classroom, put her head down, turn away from staff, stomp her feet. She may clear items/articles from desk, challenge all adult directives, change tone of voice or increase voice volume, and stop working. Once the behavior occurs, she typically comes back to her assigned area quickly and behaves appropriately without argument.

FUNCTIONAL HYPOTHESIS STATEMENT

Alice engages in this behavior to escape/avoid academic demands, teacher directions, and/or structured small- or large-group settings.

IMPRESSIONS

Strengths

- Alice is motivated by interacting with adults.

- Alice enjoys coloring and working alone at her desk.

- Alice enjoys books and having staff read with her.

- Alice enjoys walking in the hallway and visiting with family members.

- Alice can be very polite.

- Alice has a sense of humor.

- Alice can follow her daily schedule.

Areas Requiring Intervention

- Academic skills are assessed to be significantly below grade level in all areas of instruction.

- Alice needs assistance transitioning from one classroom to the next (not running in the hallway).

- Alice struggles to comply with teacher directions.

- Alice requires instruction in engaging with peers in a positive manner.

- Alice requires instruction in remaining focused in small- and large-group settings.

- Alice needs to recognize her anxiety/frustration and engage in self-calming and self-regulatory skills.

BEHAVIOR INTERVENTION PLAN

Skills Instruction

- Direct instruction focusing on Alice's daily schedule and organizational skills is needed throughout her day.

- Direct instruction is also required in the following areas:

  Transitioning from one activity to the next and out of classroom activities/events.

  Following classroom/school rules and routines.

  Following visual cue cards for behavior management strategies.

  Following Differential Reinforcement of Other Behavior (DRO), as described.

  Using a problem-solving model: (a) identify the problem, (b) generate possible solutions, (c) predict consequences of each solution, (d) choose and implement a solution, (e) evaluate outcome.

- Staff should provide social skills instruction for the following:

  Walking down the hall.

  Engaging in positive peer and adult interactions.

  Expressing frustration and anger in an appropriate manner.

  Initiating appropriate responses in a variety of situations.

- Instruction should be given to help Alice to identify other people's perceptions of her and her behaviors.

Environmental Changes

- Alice has the ability to follow a predictable routine when presented in a highly structured environment. Providing her with an individualized daily schedule provided in a visually meaningful manner will support her in transitions in the classroom as well as in other settings. A small pictorial representation (a one-inch icon), paired with a printed word, could help Alice retrieve this information quickly. This schedule should encompass all of her routines and daily activities and should be portable.

- Premacking daily events (making preferred activities contingent on completing nonpreferred activities) should be employed to increase Alice's motivation to complete academic tasks.

- Staff should use a cueing system in order to assure that they have Alice's attention prior to giving her a direction. Other guidelines: Allow additional time for Alice to process the information and wait until she is looking at staff for the direction. When it is time to transition out of the classroom, rules for transitioning in the hallway should be reviewed with Alice.

- Classroom rules/routines should be posted, pictorially and with printed word, in the classroom in the immediate vicinity of Alice's desk. These rules/routines should be reviewed each day.

- Visual cue cards, with picture and printed word, should be available to Alice. Examples of such behavioral cues are "Walking," "Quiet," "Kind words," and "Wait." Break cards (in the same format) and/or a card representing "I need to chill" should be available to Alice in all settings. An area to "chill" should be designated either in all settings or in the resource room. Currently, Alice returns to her desk area, puts her head down, and self-calms. As necessary, a barrier (portable office) may be provided to decrease distractions. When Alice chooses to take a break (activity to engage in during a break should be defined) or to "chill," she could be escorted back to the classroom to engage in self-calming/relaxation activities.

- A "feelings thermometer" should be constructed to support Alice in identifying her feelings throughout the school day. In addition, self-relaxation techniques should be developed with Alice to facilitate coping and tolerance strategies.

- Staff should write social stories/scripts (presented in picture format) to teach appropriate behaviors. These stories/scripts must be unique to Alice's specific situation, describe what she is to do, how she is to do it, and what others will think and feel when she is able to follow her plan.

- Throughout Alice's day, it is important to point out what she is doing and how her friends feel about it. It is also important to recognize when she is acting appropriately and when she is displaying appropriate social interactions with her peers.

Differential Reinforcement of Other Behavior (DRO)

- The day should be broken down into 45-minute intervals, four intervals per morning and four intervals per afternoon.

- At the beginning of the interval period, Alice will choose a reinforcer from a preestablished reinforcer menu and place a picture of her selection on an "I am working for ____" board.

- A puzzle will be constructed representing all items/activities on her choice board. This puzzle will be constructed as a four-piece puzzle of a desired item/activity.

- If Alice exhibits a precursor behavior, she will receive two warnings prior to NOT receiving the piece of the puzzle.

- At the beginning of the interval, staff should start the timer:

  When the timer goes off and the behavior has not occurred, show Alice the icon and say, "You followed teacher directions and made good choices, so you get a piece of the puzzle." Reset the timer.

  If the behavior has occurred, show Alice the icon and say, "You did not follow teacher directions and did not make good choices. Try again." Reset the timer.

If Alice exhibits physical aggression during the interval, she is to be directed to Mr. _____'s office and will not receive any chosen item/activity for the entire hour.

- On completion of the puzzle (four 45-minute intervals), Alice will receive her reinforcer.

Data collected on the target behavior should consist of the number of 45-minute intervals Alice earns her reinforcer.

Anticipatory Responses

- If Alice engages in any of the precursor behaviors, remind Alice what she is working for and redirect her to the activity/academic task at hand.

- Show Alice the puzzle format as a reminder.

- Cue Alice, as possible, referring to her schedule prior to transitions and high-demand activities (i.e., academic demands).

Reactive Strategies

If Alice engages in the target behavior, do the following:

- Give her five minutes time away from the activity or group, in a chair.

- Once the time away is over, review what she did (e.g., "You didn't follow teacher directions") and show her that she did not receive the puzzle piece.

- If physical aggression has occurred and/or Alice has locked herself in a bathroom stall or other area, get assistance from the office and remove/escort her to Mr. _____'s office.

- Follow school policy and procedures as appropriate.

  This plan should remain in effect for at least four weeks prior to changing any item or procedure.

References and Bibliography

Asher, S. L., Gordon, S. B., Selbst, M. C., & Cooperberg, M. (2010). *The behavior problems resource kit: Forms and procedures for identification, measurement, and intervention.* Champaign, IL: Research Press.

Alberto, P. A., & Troutman, A. C. (2012). *Applied behavior analysis for teachers* (9th ed.). Upper Saddle River, NJ: Prentice Hall.

Bateman, B. D. (2007). *From gobbledygook to clearly written annual IEP goals.* Verona, WI: Attainment.

Bateman, B. D., & Golly, A. (2013). *Why Johnny doesn't behave: Twenty tips and measurable BIPs.* Verona, WI: Attainment.

Bateman, B. D., & Herr, C. M. (2006). *How to develop legally correct and educationally useful programs* (4th ed.). Verona, WI: Attainment.

Bedell, J. (2013). *Does fluorescent light hurt autistic kids?* Retrieved June 5, 2014, from the James Bedell website, http://jamesbedell.com/blog/2013/6/26/does-fluorescent-lighting-hurt-autistic-kids

Crony, D. A., & Horner, R. H. (2003). *Building positive behavior supports systems in schools: Functional behavioral assessment.* New York: Guilford.

Donnellan, A., LaVigna, G., Negri-Shoultz, N., & Fassbender, L. (1988). *Progress without punishment: Effective approaches for learners with behavior problems.* New York: Teachers College Press.

Iacocca, L. (n.d.). Retrieved June 5, 2014, from the BrainyQuote website, www.brainyquote.com/quotes/quotes/l/leeiacocca125857.html

Kopkowski, C. (2008). *Why they leave.* Retrieved June 5, 2014, from the National Education Association website, www.nea.org/home/12630.htm

McDougal, J. L., Chafouleas, S. M., & Waterman, B. (2006). *Functional assessment and interventions in schools: A practitioner's guide.* Champaign, IL: Research Press.

Melograno, V. (2002). *Train the trainer certificate program: How adults learn and how to design and evaluate effective training.* Unpublished manuscript, Cleveland State University, Division of Continuing Education.

Premack, A. J., & Premack, D. (1972). Teaching language to an ape. *Scientific American, 227*(4), 92–99.

Riggs, L. (2013). *Why do teachers quit? And why do they stay?* Retrieved June 5, 2013 from the Atlantic Magazine website, www.theatlantic.com/education/archive/2013/10/why-do-teachers-quit/280699

Sorhagen, N. S. (2013). Early teacher expectations disproportionately affect poor children's high school performance. *Journal of Educational Psychology, 105*(2), 465–477.

Stipek, D. (2002). *Motivation to learn: Integrating theory and practice.* Needham Heights, MA: Allyn and Bacon.

Wright, J. (2007). *RTI toolkit: A practical guide for schools.* Port Chester, NY: Dude Publishing.

About the Author

Prior to retiring in 2005, Terri Chiara Johnston, PhD, was an educator for almost 40 years, serving as teacher, school psychologist, and program director/principal. She taught at the kindergarten and middle school level early in her career, but her passion became helping youngsters who experienced severe behavior and communication challenges. During her professional journey, she received extensive training in applied behavior analysis, structured teaching (TEACCH), and crisis management. A recognized expert in the area of autism and emotional disturbance, Terri founded a consulting company, Support 4 Teachers and Families (www.s4ts4f.com).

Now Terri is completely retired from education and enjoys life with her husband, Joe Czup, and her golden retriever therapy dog, Roux. She works as a freelance writer and stringer reporter for Northeast Ohio Media Group, writing community stories for the Cleveland *Sun News* and *cleveland.com*.